MANAGING YOUR HOUSEHOLDS WELL

Chap Bettis offers invaluable insight into an often-overlooked qualification for church leadership—the leader's homelife. Drawing from biblical wisdom and practical experience, Bettis demonstrates how family leadership develops essential skills that translate directly to church leadership. The book's concise approach and practical self-evaluation tools, including thoughtful questions for both leaders and their wives, make this an indispensable resource for current church leaders, those in training, and those responsible for developing future leaders. This is the practical guidance many of us have been waiting for.
—**Trent Casto**, Senior Pastor, Covenant Presbyterian Church, Naples, Florida

This is a good and much-needed book on a subject that, though clearly laid out in Scripture, has been too often neglected and overlooked. Every pastor or prospective pastor will benefit from reading and considering it.
—**Tim Challies**, Blogger, www.challies.com

There is a great misunderstanding over a pastor's qualifications in regard to his homelife. This is why I'm grateful that Chap Bettis wrote *Managing Your Households Well.* This book is a clear, careful, biblical, and balanced resource in regard to an essential category of a pastor's calling—his homelife. The chapters that address, with charity and grace, the behavior of the pastor's children are worth the price of the book alone. Pastors, I commend this to you.
—**Brian Croft**, Executive Director, Practical Shepherding

Christian leaders and aspiring Christian leaders have needed a book like this for a long time. Not only does Chap Bettis unpack the biblical qualifications for faithful spiritual authority, but he also explains how leadership in the home trains men to lead in the church. He speaks from a thorough understanding of Scripture and decades as a pastor. This is an essential book for your church's leadership team

and should be a required text in pastoral studies at Christian colleges and seminaries.
—**Daniel Darling**, Director, Land Center for Cultural Engagement, Southwestern Baptist Theological Seminary

I opened this book with some trepidation because I dislike being berated or barraged with instructions. Instead, I found encouragement laid out in a clear, biblical portrait of a faithful father and pastor —the kind I would like to be. Bettis offers accessible and attainable instruction from Scripture but not a low bar. He honors the nobility of pastoring and fathering and builds up the reader. I particularly appreciated the clear link between faithful shepherding in the home and in the church. It was logical, personal, and biblical. I would recommend this book to any young or aspiring pastor and elder.
—**Barnabas Piper**, Pastor, Immanuel Church, Nashville

Chap Bettis does an outstanding job of highlighting one misunderstood but key component to biblical eldership—managing one's own household well—and showing how household leadership connects with the leadership of the local church, the household of God. Leading a local church is more like leading a family than leading a business. This book should be a required training tool for preparing future pastoral elders.
—**Alexander Strauch**, Author, *Biblical Eldership*

MANAGING YOUR HOUSEHOLDS WELL

How Family Leadership Trains You for
CHURCH LEADERSHIP

CHAP BETTIS

P.O. BOX 817 • PHILLIPSBURG • NEW JERSEY 08865-0817

Italics within Scripture quotations indicate emphasis added.

Cover design by Jelena Mirkovic

Printed in the United States of America

Library of Congress Cataloging-in-Publication Data

Names: Bettis, Chap, author.
Title: Managing your households well : how family leadership trains you for church leadership / Chap Bettis.
Description: Phillipsburg : P&R Publishing, 2025. | Summary: "Men who serve the church well are men who have learned how to lead their own families with wisdom and skill. Bettis considers practical lessons from household management and debunks misconceptions"-- Provided by publisher.
Identifiers: LCCN 2024018099 | ISBN 9798887790503 (paperback) | ISBN 9798887790510 (epub)
Subjects: LCSH: Christian leadership. | Men in church work. | Parenting--Religious aspects--Christianity. | Families--Religious life.
Classification: LCC BV652.1 .B48 2024 | DDC 253--dc23/eng/20240521
LC record available at https://lccn.loc.gov/2024018099

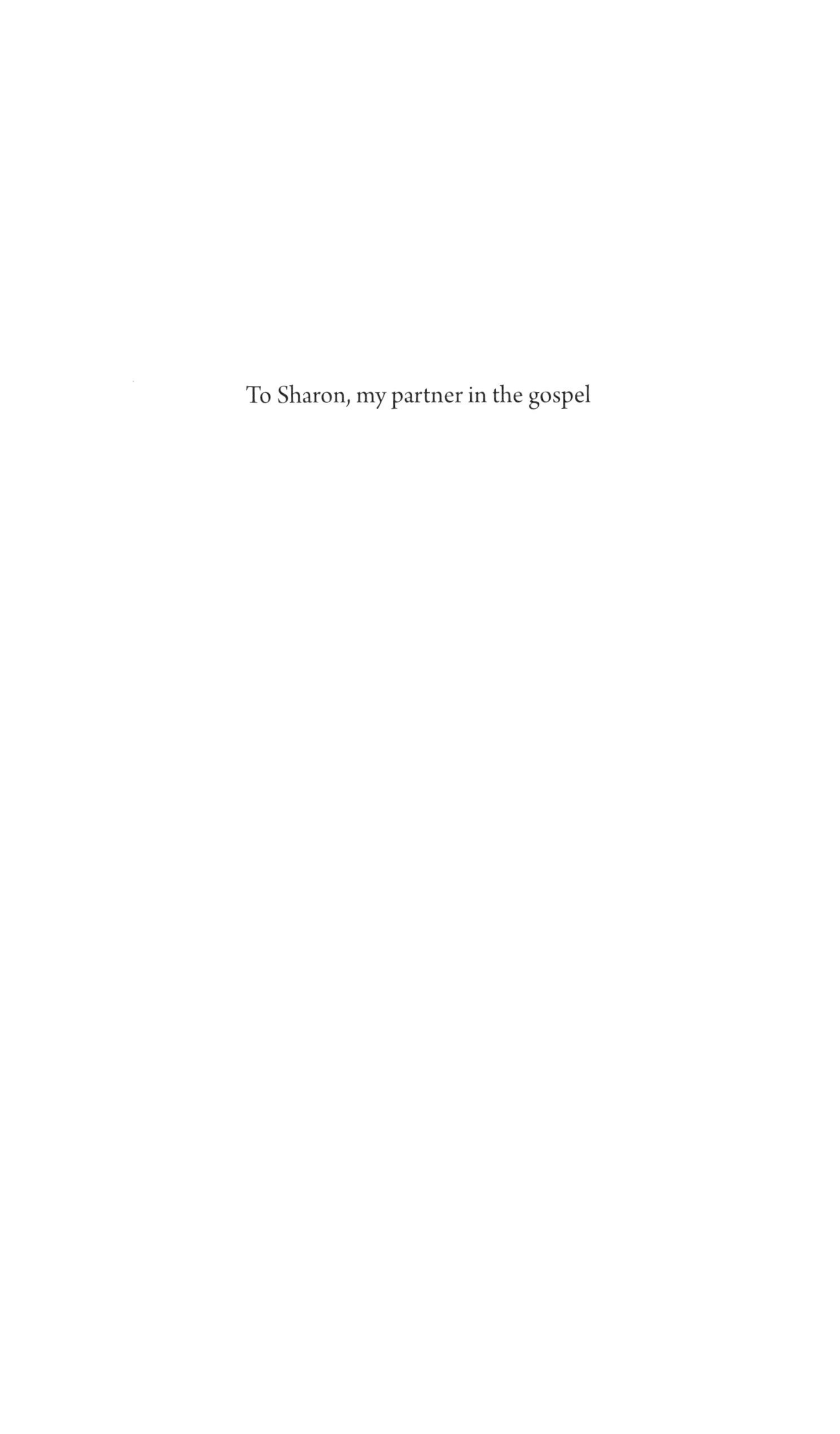

To Sharon, my partner in the gospel

Bonus resources for leading your home well and passing the gospel on to your children can be found at www.thedisciplemakingparent.com/myhwbonuses.

CONTENTS

INTRODUCTION

Jake was an energetic, smiling young pastor, fresh out of seminary with a strong vision and an abundance of ideas. His preaching was clear and true to Scripture. The small church felt blessed to have him. There was only one problem: His young children were out of control. Not by a little but by a lot—and everybody knew it. A few of the other leaders had gently tried to say something, but he would not listen to even the simplest suggestion. "Kids will be kids," he said, "and I'm going to have fun with them." Unfortunately, these leadership deficiencies eventually came out in other ways. Looking back, the church realized they had never asked questions about his homelife.

The other elders were counting the days until Ron's term as an elder was over. He could be charming to others, but behind closed doors he seemed to disagree with each new proposal that came to the group. He was, in a word, argumentative. Of course, his wife had tried to point that out when they were first married. But he wouldn't listen to her. Now she just smiles weakly and tries not to make waves. Ron's children have long since stopped talking with him about anything significant, since their dad is "always right." Too bad the church selection team had not detected this problem before they nominated him to the board.

Will was kind and easygoing. In addition, his good looks and his ready smile seemed to regularly open doors for him to take on positions of leadership. Most recently, he had been recruited to be the coach of the church basketball team. The only problem? Once in that position, he didn't coach. In fact, in the most recent game, he never even directed the team or called for substitutes. It wasn't deliberate selfishness. He was just clueless. Maybe that explained why his wife always looked so exhausted from chasing after their little children.

LEADING UNDER JESUS

What do each of these fictional but true-to-life stories have in common? Problems with leadership. Each reflects a deficiency of character in the leader that first manifested itself in the home. Then it showed up in the church. The poor leadership resulted in pain and disillusionment for the Christians under the leader's care. Why?

Good leaders bless the saints underneath them. Poor leaders hurt them.

God's people deserve and need skillful leaders. Jesus, the Anointed One, suffered and died for us on the cross and was raised for us. Afterward, the disciples saw him ascend into heaven, and Scripture tells us he was installed as the reigning King (see Ps. 2:6; Dan. 7:13–14). The kingdom is partially here, and the rule of the King has begun! He has appointed shepherd-leaders to act in his name and care for his sheep. When these leaders lead poorly, the flock suffers (see Ezek. 34:1–6). But when they shepherd well, God's people are blessed. We see this most clearly during the time of David and Solomon, Israel's golden age. It was said of David that he "shepherded them with integrity of heart; with skillful hands he led them" (Ps. 78:72 NIV). As a result, God's people flourished.

Yet all too often God's people are not flourishing. Although many leaders are earnest and well-intentioned, you probably have your own experiences with poor leadership. Or maybe you have not experienced *poor* leadership but have endured merely *passable* leadership—not terrible, but not excellent either. In addition, you may have concerns about your own leadership and be wondering how to improve.

KNOWLEDGE AND WISDOM

One reason God's people have so much poor or merely passable oversight is because we often have not pursued *leadership wisdom*. In this digital age, we confuse knowledge and wisdom. Knowledge is information, while wisdom is information aptly applied to a situation. It is skillful living. Leaders must have knowledge. But they also need wisdom and wisdom of a particular type—relational wisdom. It takes wisdom to build a family and wisdom to build a church family (see Prov. 24:3).

Where do we get this wisdom? Many seminaries do an excellent job of teaching the knowledge of Scripture but struggle to teach the wisdom that is needed to oversee the flock. That's not their fault. It's not what an academic institution is designed for. But as a result we graduate men who know the Scriptures but don't know people.

Some have attempted to address this leadership problem by looking to the world of business. Others have rightly rejected the syncretism of applying business principles to caring for God's church. But a wholesale rejection of leadership principles leaves a void. When we fail to mine Scripture for its rich teaching on leadership or de-emphasize this aspect of pastoring, those in our care may be hurt.[1]

This is unacceptable. My heart's desire is that the reigning Shepherd-King would work in his undershepherds so that we may lead God's people with integrity of heart and skillful hands.

LOOKING TO GOD'S WORD

Where do we find the training we need to skillfully lead God's people? In God's all-sufficient Word, of course! Numerous books have

1. See Albert Mohler, *The Conviction to Lead: 25 Principles for Leadership That Matters* (Bethany House, 2012), 19, in which Mohler divides the evangelical world into Believers and Leaders: "The Believers are driven by deep and passionate beliefs. . . . The problem is, many of them are not ready to lead. . . . The Leaders, on the other hand, are passionate about leadership. . . . The problem is, many of them are not sure what they believe or why it matters."

focused our attention on the priority and health of the local church; these have included a number of helpful books on selecting good men to lead.[2] However, I fear that one vital aspect of godly leadership is being overlooked. Properly understood, its recovery could have profound implications for the contemporary church.

In the middle of his teaching on elders, Paul writes of the following requirement:

> He must manage his own household well, with all dignity keeping his children submissive, for if someone does not know how to manage his own household, how will he care for God's church? (1 Tim. 3:4–5)

In these two short verses, God connects how a man leads at home with how he leads in the church. This makes clear that the family is a vital training and testing ground for church leaders. It is your first field of ministry that must be cultivated. God intends you to develop and display in your family the relational wisdom you need to lead God's people.

RESULTS OF THIS OVERSIGHT

When our seminaries and churches overlook this teaching, a number of leadership and shepherding issues can arise.

We have young pastors who can exegete a passage but don't know how to exegete people. These men equate pastoring with preaching. They lead and shepherd in a clumsy way, hurting the sheep in the process. Their preaching, although theologically sound, may be delivered in a way that doesn't connect with the heart. This lack of shepherding skill may generate conflict in a formerly peaceful church.

2. See Jeramie Rinne, *Church Elders: How to Shepherd God's People Like Jesus* (Crossway, 2014); and Alexander Strauch, *Biblical Eldership: An Urgent Call to Restore Biblical Church Leadership*, 3rd ed. (Lewis and Roth, 1995).

We are clumsy in our leadership training. Leading a church well requires an enormous amount of skill. After all, we are leading a group of volunteers who often have strong opinions about theological beliefs or ministry philosophies. We send men out to lead whose only leadership training has been one class they took in seminary. We are told that if they preach the Word correctly, the rest will take care of itself. That's refuted simply by looking at our key verse. Paul expected his leaders to be overseeing their churches and their families. And could this be why so many seminary graduates are not pastoring after five years? They have not been trained to lead, and so they grow discouraged.

We have a godliness disconnect between church life and homelife. Home is the first place to live out the gospel—and it's the hardest. Our family members are our nearest neighbors. Yet often we don't equip our congregation for family life. Troubled marriages stay troubled. Sin in the home remains hidden and unchallenged. As we recover the idea of leading our families well, we will also begin to think about better equipping the families in our churches.

We do not see the church as the "household of God" (1 Tim. 3:15). Unfortunately, Christians sometimes view the church merely as a provider of truth. However, throughout Scripture we see that the people of God are the *family* of God. Families are highly relational. The church is to be a household led by those who are spiritual fathers and examples.

MY JOURNEY

When I planted and pastored a church in New England thirty years ago, I was a decent student of the Word. But I was a terrible student of people. I was simplistic in my counsel and reserved in my demeanor. Gradually, I started to mature as a leader in my church and my family.

The Lord helped me become a more astute student of people. My sermons deepened as I gained more insight into the struggles common to Christians. My biblical counsel became more realistic and compassionate. Though still an introvert, I was learning to listen, emotionally connect, and encourage. I became better able to lead wisely, lovingly, and effectively in both my home and the church.

This didn't mean our home was free of problems or stress. Having four children in six years was both wonderfully sweet and gloriously chaotic. Six sinners living together under a small roof meant lots of sinful disturbances and sparks.

But during this time, I discovered that as I became a better husband and dad, I also became a better pastor. And as I became a better pastor, I also became a better husband and dad. There was a vital interplay between these two worlds. They were not the same, but they were similar. As I was learning to lead my smaller household, I was also learning to lead the larger household of God. It was like learning to fly on a small Piper Cub airplane before getting behind the controls of a commercial aircraft.

DEVELOPING RELATIONAL WISDOM

In what follows, you will discover some of the ties between leading your smaller household and leading God's larger household. This resource is not meant to be a comprehensive leadership book. Nor is it meant to go into depth on marriage or child-rearing. Instead, it is meant to make clear the connection between leading your family well and leading God's people well. God has given you a family to help you *develop* your leadership and shepherding wisdom. And God has given you a family to *display* your leadership and shepherding wisdom. My hope is that you will glean lessons you might be missing.

You don't need to be married to learn these lessons. A man does not need to be a father, or even a husband, to serve as an elder.[3]

3. A man who is unmarried could be still qualified for eldership. He would just need to be sensitive to some blind spots he might have. However, a married man who has deliberately chosen to be childless for the sake of career advancement should be challenged. Children are one of God's purposes for marriage.

Paul, who wrote the qualifications for elders, was not married. Many single brothers have served and do serve the church well. Marriage and fatherhood are not the only opportunities to gain the relational wisdom a leader needs. I learned plenty of leadership lessons through mistakes on the job. Nor does being married and having children automatically grant you this wisdom. I have met a number of men who are husbands and fathers but who have not grasped the lessons on the following pages. However, a family *is* the perfect place to learn some of these principles.

THEOLOGICAL FOUNDATIONS AND PRACTICAL APPLICATIONS

This resource is broken into two sections. In part 1, we will look at the theological foundations for leading our households well. Chapter 1 is an introduction to biblical offices in the church. In chapter 2, we will dive deeply into what Paul meant in 1 Timothy 3:4–5 when he said that we are to manage well. Chapter 3 will take a close look at Titus 1:6, the parallel passage to our text in 1 Timothy. In chapter 4, we will think about what happens when a leader and his family hit a storm.

Part 2 of the book will help us think about other practical lessons we can learn from leading our families. In chapter 5, we will consider leading and overseeing well. In chapter 6, we will think about how we can become more skillful communicators. Conflict and unity are the subjects of chapter 7. Chapter 8 will help us think about how God can grow our character. Our conclusion will discuss why God wants us to lead well. In addition, appendix A contains an important overview of what godly leadership actually is. Appendices B and C include evaluations for you and your wife to complete.

WHO WILL BENEFIT?

It is easy to skip over the subject of leading your family well if you are not a pastor or an aspiring pastor. Yet I believe there are various categories of people who will be challenged and edified by considering this subject.

1. *Husbands and dads.* As we will see shortly, managing your household well is a qualification for elders and deacons. But does that let the rest of us off the hook? No! The first place all of us live out the gospel is in our homes. As we love and lead our wives and our children, we will display the gospel to a broken world. All of us can grow in this area.

2. *Current pastors and elders, young and old.* If you are currently serving as a church shepherd, I want to remind you of this qualification for your office. Increased attention to shepherding your family can increase your leadership competency and deepen your wisdom. My prayer is that entire church leadership teams would study this resource and challenge one another to grow in wisdom.

3. *Current deacons.* This aspect of godliness is for deacons as well. Even if you don't have any shepherding duties at this time, you can still learn the principles of oversight. And as an officer, your home should display the gospel to others. Paul specifically states that you are to manage your household well.

4. *Current ministry leaders without the title of pastor or deacon.* There are many influential leadership roles throughout a church that do not have the title of pastor or deacon. Small group leaders, life group leaders, and ministry team leaders are just a few of these crucial roles. You are vital to a ministry's flourishing, and so these lessons apply to you too.

5. *Aspiring elders, deacons, and ministry leaders.* If you desire to be a ministry leader in a church or a parachurch ministry, praise God! Every church needs more godly, skilled, and wise leaders. You can learn many lessons in your home right now.

6. Current seminarians. Perhaps you are hoping to one day lead the people of God and are training for that role now. You need wisdom to lead well. Yes, the church is the pillar and foundation of the truth, but she is also God's household. Family leadership is often a blind spot for students. A dean of one prominent seminary remarked to me, "Preparation for ministry is seen as unrelated to leading a family. Young men are checked out when it comes to their homelife." This should not be! God is training you in the classroom *and* in the home.

7. Leaders with prodigals. Because Titus 1:6 has been misunderstood, many have believed that if they have a child who has walked away from the faith, they have not managed their households well. This wrong view is like rubbing salt into an open wound. I hope chapters 3 and 4 will be a balm for your soul.

8. Interested women. Lastly, I hope women will benefit from this short resource. Because you are made in his image, God has also called you to manage well in the spheres in which you find yourself (see Prov. 31:10–31; 1 Tim. 5:14). In addition, if you are married to a church officer, it would be good to think about how you might encourage your husband to grow in this calling. Though this short work is written by a man and specifically aimed at men, I think you will benefit from reading it.

CONCLUSION

God's household deserves the wisest and best leadership possible. Your family deserves that as well. The Lord has created a marvelous pipeline in which lessons learned in one sphere often transfer to the other. Let's study together how both can display the love of God and the glory of God to a watching world.

FOR REFLECTION AND APPLICATION

1. When in your life have you experienced poor leadership? What was the problem? How did it impact you?
2. Have you served under any excellent leaders? What made them such good leaders?
3. What do you think of the distinction between knowledge and wisdom? Had you thought of that before? What difference should this distinction make in your leadership going forward?
4. Have you considered that your authority comes from King Jesus? What difference does that make in how you exercise your influence?
5. Which category or categories do you fit in as one who will benefit from reading this book? What are you hoping to gain from this investment of time and attention?

PART 1

THEOLOGICAL FOUNDATIONS

1

MANAGING YOUR HOUSEHOLD WELL

And David shepherded them with integrity of heart; with skillful hands he led them. (Ps. 78:72 NIV)

"Would you come to my ordination as a pastor?"

I was finishing up a year of teaching at a Christian school. Though I was genuinely interested in having a few of my friends and fellow teachers attend, my eye was really on the cute second-grade teacher. She and I had recently been on a few dates that seemed to have gone well. As I spent time with her, she appeared to have a heart for ministry, and I was hoping she also had a heart for me. But at this moment in time, that was not clear. Thankfully, everyone accepted the invitation. On June 28, 1987, I was ordained as a pastor, and a little over a year later, I married that second-grade teacher. And thus began the adventure of learning to care for God's family and my family.

Whether in the church or in the family, people need leaders. Overseeing God's people can be a humbling and sacrificial way of serving, but it is also a high privilege. If you are called to care in this manner, then leading is one way you express your love for Jesus, just as it was for Peter (see John 21:15–17).

Leadership is so important that the Lord gives specific instructions about it throughout his Word. What are we to look for in a leader? This is not left to our speculation. First Timothy 3:1–13 and Titus 1:5–9 clearly present the qualifications for church leaders. The church is to have two offices: elders, or pastors, and deacons. And since Christians are to imitate their leaders, the character of those individuals is vitally important.

THE QUALITIES OF A NEW TESTAMENT OFFICER

While the full text of 1 Timothy 3:1–13 is worth meditating on, we'll focus on the following verses:

> The saying is trustworthy: If anyone aspires to the office of overseer, he desires a noble task. Therefore an overseer must be above reproach. (vv. 1–2)

> He must manage his own household well, with all dignity keeping his children submissive, for if someone does not know how to manage his own household, how will he care for God's church? (vv. 4–5)

> Let deacons each be the husband of one wife, managing their children and their own households well. (v. 12)

The same household qualification for elders is also mentioned in Titus 1:5–7, and in this case, it is actually listed first. Paul gave Titus this instruction:

> The reason I left you in Crete was to set right what was left undone and, as I directed you, to appoint elders in every town. An elder must be blameless, the husband of one wife, with

> faithful children who are not accused of wildness or rebellion. As an overseer of God's household, he must be blameless. (CSB)

We will spend the rest of this book exploring the meaning and application of these verses. But one thing is very clear: You demonstrate your spiritual maturity in part by how you lead in your home. God is serious about how we love and lead both our wives and our children. The power of the gospel should be most evident in how we treat those closest to us. If we cannot love them, how can we love others?

Why would Paul emphasize household leadership when looking for leaders in the church? Why not emphasize a man's business or civic achievements? There are many reasons, but one has to do with recovering an overlooked New Testament term for *leader*.

THE ELDER-OVERSEER

The New Testament uses a number of words to refer to men who lead the church. They are called *shepherds*, from which we get our word *pastor*. They shepherd underneath the Chief Shepherd (see 1 Peter 5:4). This term emphasizes the leader's role in feeding and guarding his people. The leaders are also called *elders*. This term emphasizes the maturity required to lead as well as the duty of these men to serve as examples for the flock.[1]

But there is another biblical term for leaders that we rarely see today: *overseers*. This term leads off our passage in 1 Timothy: "If anyone aspires to the office of overseer . . ." (3:1). In another passage, Paul charges the Ephesian elders to "pay careful attention to yourselves and to all the flock, in which the Holy Spirit has made you overseers" (Acts 20:28). He addresses the leadership at Philippi as "the overseers and

1. The term *pastor* or *shepherd* is found in Ephesians 4:11. It is used along with *overseer* in 1 Peter 2:25. *Overseer* is found in Philippians 1:1 and 1 Timothy 3:1–7. It is used along with *elder* in Titus 1:5–7. *Elder* is used in Acts 11:30; 14:23; 15:2–23; 16:4; 21:18; and 1 Timothy 5:17–19. This kind of language is used in Acts 20:17–28 and 1 Peter 5:1–5.

deacons" (Phil. 1:1). Writing to Titus, Paul says, "An overseer, as God's steward, must be above reproach" (Titus 1:7). Paul then reemphasizes the point by calling such leaders God's stewards. *Oikonomos,* translated as "steward," is the Greek word for "house manager," the representative who watches over an owner's possessions.

These three terms—*elder, pastor, overseer*—describe the same function of leadership. Though they have slightly different shades of meaning, the terms are complementary, and Scripture uses them interchangeably. It would be proper for us to speak of pastor-overseers or elder-overseers in our context today.

OVERSEEING GOD'S HOUSEHOLD

What does a pastor-elder-overseer actually oversee? The New Testament uses several different metaphors to describe the church. But one metaphor is particularly prominent in 1 Timothy and indeed throughout the New Testament as a whole. After detailing the need for elders and deacons to manage their households well, Paul immediately includes this purpose statement for the whole letter of 1 Timothy:

> I am writing these things to you so that, if I delay, you may know how one ought to behave in the household of God, which is the church of the living God, a pillar and buttress of the truth. (3:14–15)

Paul calls the church the household of God. He continues this family imagery later in the letter when he instructs Timothy to treat older men, older women, younger men, and younger women as fathers, mothers, brothers, and sisters, respectively (see 1 Tim. 5:1–2). If you think about how many times the imagery of brothers and sisters is used in the New Testament, you could argue that a household or a family is, in fact, the predominant metaphor for the church!

Just as an actual shepherd watches over sheep to see that they are prospering, well-fed, well-watered, and defended, so God's overseers watch over the church to see that the members of God's household are spiritually prospering. They ensure that God's family is nourished, protected, well-ordered, and directed. Shepherd-overseers steward God's people underneath the authority of the Overseer of our souls (see 1 Peter 2:25).

MANAGING A SMALLER HOUSEHOLD

Once we understand that the church is a family-household, we can immediately understand why God would look to see how a person is managing a smaller household. Paul draws a direct line of connection: "If someone does not know how to manage his own household, how will he care for God's church?" (1 Tim. 3:5).

Commenting on this verse, John Calvin wrote, "This argument, drawn from the less to the greater, is in itself manifest, that he who is unfit for governing a family will be altogether unable to govern a people."[2] In other words, how can a man care for God's larger, more complex family if he cannot manage his smaller, simpler one? His failure to lead well in his home proves that he will not be able to oversee God's family.

In his letter to Titus, Paul begins a parallel passage by highlighting domestic oversight. Is a potential church overseer devoted to his wife? Does he care for his children well? While in 1 Timothy domestic qualities come after a number of qualifications relating to personal character, they lead the way in Titus. Surely, the space devoted to such qualities in both 1 Timothy 3 and Titus 1 demonstrates how important they are to the Lord. God cares about how we lead and love in our homes!

Paul repeats these domestic qualities when he speaks of the other set of church officers, deacons: "Let deacons each be the husband of one wife, managing their children and their own households well"

2. John Calvin, "The Epistles to Timothy, Titus and Philemon," in *Calvin's Commentaries*, vol. 21, *Galatians, Ephesians, Philippians, Colossians, I & II Thess, I & II Timothy, Titus, Philemon*, trans. John King (Baker, 1974), 83.

(1 Tim. 3:12). From this repetition we can infer that leadership in the home is a mark of spiritual maturity for all men.

As individuals made in God's likeness, we image him as we rule over the different areas he has given to us (see Gen. 1:28; 2:15). We care for the earthly fields that he has entrusted to us even as we are trained to reign for eternity. When we cultivate order and beauty in those areas, we bring him glory. Thus, not only officers but all men and women should aim to manage their households well as they pursue Christlikeness.

NOT TO BE OVERSTATED

Perhaps we need some qualification here. A family is not a church, and leading a family is less complex than shepherding a church. But these passages are clear and incontrovertible: God wants his officers to lead their homes well. In order to influence any group of people, a leader must learn how to relate to people effectively. How can we grow in those skills? Paul makes clear that one place we develop and demonstrate that relational wisdom is in our homes.

Learning to lead the members of your family will make you better able to oversee members of your church. Similarly, the lessons you grasp while leading the flock should make you a better husband and father. A plumber might not make deep connections between his job and his family (other than fixing the pipes!), but a church leader should see profound similarities.

WHAT DOES *MANAGE* MEAN?

Having understood the importance of 1 Timothy 3:4–5, let's go deeper. What does it mean to *manage*?

We often pit the concept of managing against that of leading: "People work for managers; they follow leaders." Leadership, we are told, is exciting and visionary. Management is necessary but dull. In the business world, the word *leader* carries status, while the term *manager* does not. Everyone wants to be a thought leader. No one wants to be a thought manager.

But what is the meaning of the word in the original Greek? Does it carry the same connotations as our English word *manage*? When we survey our English Bibles, we find the Greek word *proistémi* translated with many different words for leadership. Most modern versions translate the word *proistémi* in 1 Timothy 3:4, 5, and 12 as "manage." However, Paul uses the same word for elders in 1 Timothy 5:17, where many versions translate it as "rule."

> Let the elders who *rule* well be considered worthy of double honor, especially those who labor in preaching and teaching. (1 Tim. 5:17)

In Romans 12:8, the same word is traditionally translated as "leads." In 1 Thessalonians 5:12, Paul again uses *proistémi* in conjunction with leaders, and we read about "those who . . . *are over you* in the Lord." Thus we see that, while the English words *manage, rule,* and *lead* all carry slightly different connotations, they translate the same word and concept in the original Greek. The primary meaning of this word is to lead or govern. We will be using the words *lead* and *manage* interchangeably, as these English connotations are represented in *proistémi.*

LEADING AND CARING

We should note that *proistémi* also carries the meaning of protecting or caring for one's charges while leading them.[3] This is especially obvious in 1 Timothy 3:5. Given that Paul is setting up a parallel comparison, we would expect him to say if a man cannot *manage* his own household, how will he *manage* the church of God?

3. See William D. Mounce, *Word Biblical Commentary*, ed. Bruce M. Metzger, David A. Hubbard, and Glenn W. Barker, vol. 46, *Pastoral Epistles*, ed. Ralph P. Martin and Lynn Allan Losie (Thomas Nelson, 2000), 178.

Instead, Paul highlights the aspect of care in leadership. In fact, the word itself includes this very concept. Jesus uses the same Greek word to describe how the Good Samaritan oversaw and cared for the wounded man on the side of the road (see Luke 10:34). Thus, elders and deacons, and, by implication, mature men, are to demonstrate leadership that is both caring and devoted—in other words, loving leadership.

IS IT POSSIBLE TO MANAGE WELL?

Having introduced the idea of leading our families, let's ask, "Is it even possible to manage well?" You may be tempted to react to 1 Timothy 3:5, and even to the title of this book, with guilt or an eye roll. "Who can possibly manage his family well?" I remember the chaos in our household the year we had a seven-, five-, three-, and one-year-old. It sure didn't feel like I was managing well during that time. I was merely trying to survive! Or did I manage well when we had four teenagers and life felt like we were riding through Class V rapids?

The very fact that God requires this quality for leaders means he expects that men can achieve it. The verse states that we are to manage *well,* not manage *perfectly*. Leading well does not mean having a family without problems. If God puts it in his Word, then it must be possible. Empowered by the Spirit, all mature Christian men can and should care for their households well.

CONCLUSION

Jesus said, "One who is faithful in a very little is also faithful in much" (Luke 16:10). Leading God's people is a privilege. A wise, caring, godly leader is worth his weight in gold. God has given the home in part to help us see if a man will lead well. And God has given us the home to help *train* us to lead well.

FOR REFLECTION AND APPLICATION

1. How does this chapter challenge or expand your understanding of godly leadership?
2. How might your view of leaders change if we called them overseers?
3. When you think of your church, do you think of it as God's family and household? What implications do these metaphors have for your interactions with the people in your church? How does it affect your view of God's people?
4. Consider the additional nuance of leading as "caring for." How does this connotation correct some common misunderstandings of leadership?
5. Have you skimmed past the verses discussed in this chapter because they seemed impossible to fulfill? How does this chapter strengthen your resolve to understand them?

2

KEEPING YOUR CHILDREN SUBMISSIVE WITH ALL DIGNITY

. . . with all dignity keeping his children submissive . . . (*1 Tim. 3:4*)

Jake, Ron, and Will from our introduction are all examples of leadership that harms God's people. Jake's permissiveness, Ron's contentiousness, and Will's passivity exemplify leadership that is detrimental. Were there clues missed along the way that could have prevented these problems? The answer to that question is a resounding "Yes!" Wisdom would have come by focusing on our key qualification for church officers. In the next several chapters, we will seek to properly understand the relevant important Scriptures in order to determine whether a man has the relational wisdom to lead.

To make such a determination, Paul directs us to consider how a man is doing as a father-overseer of his household. But then Paul zeroes in on one specific aspect of household oversight: how a man interacts with his children. Finally, Paul narrows it down to an even smaller subset of parenting: training children to obey.[1]

1. This focus does not downplay a godly man's love and care for his wife, which is described and commanded in other places in Scripture. We will cover other aspects of loving and leading one's family later in the book.

In 1 Timothy 3:4, Paul focuses on how a godly man actively trains his children to comply with his instructions. Other translations convey this idea. An elder is to "have his children under control with all dignity" (CSB) or "see that his children obey him with proper respect" (NIV).

In part 2, we will examine other aspects of loving and leading a family and how those can train us for ministry leadership. But in this chapter, we will place our focus where Paul does—on the obedience of our children.

MISAPPLICATIONS

Historically, Paul's instruction for leaders to see that their children obey them has been wielded carelessly by church members. Both leaders and their children have been hurt. Men have even lost their jobs after members referenced this verse! As a result of its misuse, this Scripture has fallen out of favor, and today it is often overlooked or ignored. In addition, parenting is deeply personal. Parents are often not open to correction or evaluation because it reflects on them. Let's rectify those issues by thinking clearly about what Paul is *not* saying here. It might relieve the stress that we put on our children and on ourselves.

First, managing our households well does not mean that our homes are serene and problem free. Anytime sinners live with other sinners, there will be complications. Sometimes, as parents, we can hold expectations that are too high. We put pressure on our children. Because they represent us, we desire for them to be obedient in public and not to embarrass us. We want our older children to be spiritually mature or our younger children to know all the answers in Sunday school. And when they don't meet our expectations, we are disappointed or angry. This pressure on our children can originate in our own hearts.[2]

Second, managing well does not mean that our children live up to the expectations of others. Sometimes this pressure for well-mannered

2. See Barnabas Piper, *The Pastor's Kid: Finding Your Own Faith and Identity* (David C Cook, 2014), for some of the unique temptations that dads who are pastors may face.

children comes from the older saints in the church. Pastors' kids often report that they have felt watched by many in the congregation. They sensed an obligation to behave perfectly all the time. Thank heavens my church did not have this attitude. I remember a day when the Sunday school teacher reported that our three-year-old daughter had spent the time hitting all the boys during class. Sharon and I had some work to do! But these teachers understood that children are . . . children and that this instance of poor behavior did not characterize our daughter or our parenting in general.

Third, managing our households well does not mean that church leaders never sin in our dealings at home. There are no perfect parents. Instead, a home that displays the gospel is one in which Dad and Mom see their weaknesses and rely on Jesus's power and wisdom. They see their need for his forgiveness. These imperfect parents are living in the tension of being both authorities in the home and sinners in need of grace.

Although 1 Timothy 3:4 has been misapplied, we dare not overlook it. It speaks directly to our day. Indeed, it is all too common to see young pastors who are passive and permissive in their leadership because they want to be their children's friend. Perhaps they think authority and discipline will squelch their kids' spirits. These young men excuse their children when they run wild, speak disrespectfully, and ignore clear commands. The older saints are not always wrong when they worry about indulgent younger parents. Paul is speaking to exactly this issue of permissiveness.

KEEPING YOUR CHILDREN SUBMISSIVE

In 1 Timothy 3, Paul says that we can detect mature godliness in a man who is *keeping his children submissive*. Wow! This sounds so countercultural that it's almost painful to write the sentence. It sounds like medieval thinking.

However, Paul's point is clear: A godly Christian father will exercise his authority in a way that will lead his children to obey him.

He realizes that it is possible to have children who are obedient and respectful and that if a man has disobedient and wild young children, it reflects poorly on him. God commands our children to obey us (see Eph. 6:1–3). This means that they *can* obey and that they *should* obey. But because they are sinful, we are not surprised when they disobey. Our job, God states, is to bring our children up with the training and instruction of the Lord (see Eph. 6:4).

A wise man trusts his wife with much of the day-to-day parenting responsibilities, but he has not abdicated his role as father. He and his wife are united in their biblical philosophy.[3] A godly dad evaluates what his children can handle and, together with his wife, sets high but reasonable standards. He is aware of his children's obedience or lack thereof. He knows what rewards and consequences get results, and he makes skillful use of them. He makes it both advisable and reasonable to obey. In addition, he has captured the hearts of his children so that they generally *want* to comply.

Unfortunately, even in Christian circles, parents often neglect to train children to obey. Many seem to believe that speaking the gospel to our children is all there is to godly parenting. But a thoughtful biblical parent will both speak the gospel *and* shape the will with consequences. Children—whether or not they have given their lives to Christ—can be trained in qualities like self-control, kindness, generosity, and thoughtfulness. Although character training cannot regenerate the heart, it does shape the heart.

WITH ALL DIGNITY

We cannot leave this passage without noticing the phrase *with all dignity*. When I hear *dignified*, I think of older, quiet, and reserved individuals. My young, godly, and fun-loving pastors don't fit that description! The NIV helps us with a different wording:

3. See Chap Bettis, *Parenting with Confidence: Biblical Truth in a Chaotic World* (multimedia course, video, and workbook), for help in this area: www.thedisciplemakingparent.com/parenting-with-confidence/.

> . . . and see that his children obey him, and he must do so in a manner worthy of full respect. (1 Tim. 3:4 NIV2011)

A godly man leads his children to obey him in a manner that prompts respect from his children and others. God cares not only about the results of our training but about the manner of our training. It is possible to keep small children cowering by means of anger, manipulation, and sheer force of will, but children who are parented this way lose respect for their fathers over time. We are not representing our heavenly Father when we discipline in anger! Godly men shepherd without habitually losing their cool.

FAITHFUL, NOT WILD AND DISOBEDIENT

This brings us to Paul's parallel passage for elders in Titus 1:6: They are to have "faithful children who are not accused of wildness or rebellion" (CSB). Here, Paul paints the same picture with different words. A good leader's children who are in the home are generally faithful to their father. They are not living wild and out-of-control lives right under their father's nose. We expect a godly man to be connected to his teen and to carefully and lovingly bring consequences to bear on the natural challenges of the teenage years.

WHY THIS EMPHASIS?

Why does Paul emphasize a man's ability to keep his children obedient? One reason is that the gospel ought to be lived out in the home. Godly men and women desire to cultivate joyful and (generally) obedient children who reflect the Lord and serve as a witness to the world.

Paul gives us another reason as well: "For if someone does not know how to manage his own household, how will he care for God's church?" (1 Tim. 3:5). Oversight of the home, and particularly the oversight of children that results in their obedience, reveals one key trait indicating whether a man can lead in a church. John Stott comments on this passage:

> So the married pastor is called to leadership in two families, his and God's, and the former is to be the training-ground for the latter. . . . The word *manage* (4, 5) translates *proistamenos,* which is a word for "leader," combining the concepts of "rule" and "care." . . . It indicates that, although pastoral ministry is a servant ministry characterized by gentleness, a certain authority also attaches to it. One cannot expect discipline in the local church if pastors have not learned to exercise it in their home.[4]

Although I mentioned it in chapter 1, this point bears repeating: Godly church leaders are characterized by both rule and care. Stated another way, godly leaders will lead with authority and affection. Charles Spurgeon recognized that affection mingled with authority characterizes our heavenly Father.[5] This combination also characterizes godly leadership, whether the individual is parenting, pastoring, or leading a ministry team.

Let's take a closer look at a godly leader's duty to exercise authority and affection. After that, we will end by underscoring the need for authenticity in faithful leadership.

Authority

We live in an era when abuses of authority have been widely reported. As a result, there is a shadow of suspicion over nearly all forms of leadership. But wasn't Satan's first scheme to tempt Adam and Eve to question the goodness of God's rule? The answer to abusive authority is not *no* authority but *good* and *proper* authority.

4. John Stott, *Guard the Truth: The Message of 1 Timothy & Titus* (InterVarsity Press, 1996), 98.

5. See C. H. Spurgeon, "Morning, January 26," in *Morning and Evening: Daily Readings*, Christian Classics Ethereal Library, www.ccel.org/ccel/spurgeon/morneve.d0126am.html.

What is authority? Authority is the right and responsibility to command or act. A pastor's authority is his right or authorization to oversee God's people. As leaders, we are called to take people where God wants them to go, in God's manner and using God's resources. One of those resources is the authority we have been given.

Unfortunately, young leaders often have a simplistic view of this gift from God. They treat their pastoral authority as no different from that of a business CEO or a military commander. Some might expect that because they have an MDiv or bear the office of elder, they have an inherent right to rule. Unfortunately, they have confused what Jonathan Leeman calls the "authority of command" and the "authority of counsel."[6] On the one hand, a CEO or military officer exercises authority of command and rightly commands those underneath him. On the other hand, the elder's authority of counsel is earned, exercised with a lighter touch, and applied in the context of trust and relationship. As pastors, we must care for Jesus's sheep in a loving rather than domineering manner (see 1 Peter 5:3–4). And where can we learn to do that? In the home. Alexander Strauch concurs when he writes, "Caring for the local church is more like managing a family than managing a business or state. . . . A man may be a successful businessman, a capable public official, a brilliant office manager, or a top military leader, but a terrible church leader. In the family of God, a man's ability to lead his family is the test that qualifies or disqualifies a man to be an elder."[7]

Parents are called to wisely use the authority of both command and counsel. When our children are young, we start with lots of command and control. Gradually, with a steady hand and many prayers for wisdom, our authority of command should shift to mostly that of counsel. Understanding this is absolutely crucial to being a godly parent. The biological father who constantly says "I'm the

6. Jonathan Leeman, *Authority: How Godly Rule Protects the Vulnerable, Strengthens Communities, and Promotes Human Flourishing* (Crossway, 2023), 149.

7. Alexander Strauch, *Biblical Eldership: An Urgent Call to Restore Biblical Church Leadership* (Lewis and Roth, 1988), 202.

father—you will do it because I say so" may be correct in his understanding of positional authority, but he is not correct in his use of relational influence. He will quickly lose his child's heart. There are plenty of times we settle a question with younger children by stating "I'm the dad." However, as our children grow older, our listening, empathizing, reasoning, and persuading all should increase. Certainly, we can pull out the "I'm the dad" card in the teenage years, but it should become less frequent.

Similarly, young church leaders need to realize that while they may have been given positional authority, the essence of their influence is spiritual. Thus, as they grow in their understanding of God's will in his Word and in their understanding of people, they will grow in their ability to influence. This explains the difference between the godly older pastor and the new, inexperienced shepherd. While they both have the same positional authority, they do not have the same spiritual influence. This spiritual influence increases as we develop relational wisdom, biblical convictions, and sensitivity to the Spirit. Such spiritual wisdom helps me know when to hold my ground, when to compromise, when to correct, when to apologize, and when to explain. It helps me know not only the Spirit's direction but also the Spirit's timing.

The best leaders are aware of their own authority but wear it loosely. They are not domineering; instead, they are persuasive. They do the patient work of keeping the hearts of those in their churches or families. They make the hard decisions but are not constantly flaunting their authority. As Leeman observes, such a leader exercises his authority based on relationship and trust.[8] Like our dad above, these leaders oversee their households with a smile *and* a steady hand. Even as they make the hard decisions, they are seeking to help those underneath them understand their reasoning.

Certainly, there are times when we must take an unpopular stand or have a hard conversation. Perhaps, when writing this passage in

8. See Leeman, *Authority*, 160.

1 Timothy 3:4–5, Paul had in mind the disastrous behavior of Aaron. With Moses on Mount Sinai for forty days, Aaron was left in charge. And when the people desired to rebel against God, Aaron didn't oppose them—in fact, he even aided in their rebellion. Scripture records that the people were out of control because Aaron let them run wild (see Ex. 32:25).

Leading God's people where he wants them to go involves using your authority to oppose sin. Man's original call was both positive and negative. We were to work the garden and to keep or protect it (see Gen. 2:15). Good shepherds will seek to cultivate godliness *and* correct sin.

Leeman helps us both recover and think clearly about our need for this authority. Good authority, he says, is accountable to a higher authority and is neither permissive nor authoritarian, but rather life-giving. It constantly seeks wisdom and bears the cost of being a leader. This helps us understand what to look for in a potential church shepherd. Is a man's home flourishing and life-giving? Does he tend to be either permissive or authoritarian?[9]

One of the first lay elders who served in our new church plant erred toward authoritarianism. He was a big personality and a jokester, and so everyone seemed to love him. Having immersed himself in the cassette-tape ministry of a well-known preacher, he knew the Word and seemed like a perfect fit for the elder team. But once he joined the team, it didn't take long for us to realize how harsh and argumentative he was with both church members and his fellow elders. Looking back now, I realize that simply observing how he treated his wife and children would have made me more discerning. Studying his family would have helped me realize that they were merely compliant, not flourishing. He exercised his authority harshly in his home and later in the church. The wounds he inflicted in private conversations as an elder hurt many.

At the other end of the spectrum was a man I deeply admired. Others did also. That's why they selected him as an elder. But rather

9. See Leeman, 89.

than being harsh, he was passive. He was always "working on his own relationship with God." He never seemed to have the outward focus to consistently shepherd others. He held authority but would not use it for the good of the flock.

Both pastors and fathers exercise an authority delegated to them by God. A godly leader works to improve how he exercises this oversight so that it blesses the people under him and leads them to flourish.

Affection

Understanding the nature of authority is not enough. Godly leaders must also have an affection for those in their care. Genuine affection is essential in oiling the friction of both family life and church life. As the saying goes, "People don't care how much you know until they know how much you care." Affection is one way to show those in your charge that you care for them.

Where do we get this affection? From Jesus! Paul said that he yearned for the Philippian church with the affection of Christ Jesus (see Phil. 1:8). Does your view of Jesus include his affection? He felt love for people, and people felt his love. Isn't this why he was so attractive to those who were suffering? He had a joyful affection for them. To grow in Christlikeness is to grow in this tenderness for others. We cultivate this affection by praying to see others through the eyes of Jesus and asking him to increase our love for them. I have met too many church leaders who have the Word of Christ in them but not his warmth. These brothers will not be effective in God's kingdom.

Thankfully, our affection can grow over time. Paul prayed that the love of the Philippian church would abound more and more. He was praying that these individuals would have a greater capacity to love. But Paul went further and asked that their love would become more knowledgeable and discerning (see Phil. 1:9–10). In other words, that as they matured, they would love *more* and love *wiser*. The wise shepherd is also praying this for himself.

As I stated in the introduction, when I first became a pastor, I was reserved. I intimidated people, and that was fine by me. I didn't even realize that I needed to grow in love. But it was my children who melted my heart. I found myself composing little songs at their birth. I was a father, and I was overjoyed. Gradually, over time, the Lord developed me into a more tender, large-hearted, and sympathetic leader. Whether you have children or not, realizing this need can prompt you to cry out to the Lord, asking that he would enlarge your heart for those under your care.

Charles Spurgeon remarks on this requirement for a pastor: "A man who is to do much with men must love them and feel at home with them. An individual who has no geniality about him had better be an undertaker and bury the dead, for he will never succeed in influencing the living. . . . A man must have a great heart, if he would have a great congregation. . . . When a man has a large, loving heart, men go to him as ships to a haven and feel at peace when they have anchored under the lee of his friendship."[10] What is this, if not affection and love?

Authenticity

Finally, we must add one more important quality to our list: authenticity. Although Paul assumes it, we shouldn't take this key quality for granted. Even as a church leader is being studied by his flock, he is being studied by his children. When your children look at you, can they say, "He is the same person in public as he is at home"? Or do you feel the pressure to perform in one or both of these spheres? Are you realistic about both the victory you have in Christ and the sin that remains in your heart?

Studying my attitude at home helps me see how I need to grow. Since I am responsible before God for my actions and reactions, my behavior at home can reveal my true character. Charles Spurgeon concurred, and he spoke a convicting word to us fathers: "What a man is at home that he is and though he be a saint abroad, if he be a devil

10. C. H. Spurgeon, *Lectures to My Students* (Hendrickson Publishers, 2010), 66.

at home, you may depend upon it that the last is his real character."[11] In my home, God shines a floodlight on the true condition of my heart. The Lord gives us our families not only for our happiness but also so that we can grow in our holiness.

As a pastor, you live authentically by letting the flock know when you have made mistakes in the past. Or authenticity might mean apologizing for mistakes in the present. It is understanding that the grace of God both covers over sin and empowers our efforts. As a dad, my most common struggle was with impatience. Unfortunately, my children saw that sin often. As the Lord brought this area to my attention, I earnestly desired to repent. How? I sought to hold myself to a high standard of godliness, ask forgiveness of my children when I fell short, and take practical steps to change. I wanted my children to know that I was working on this part of my life. Living authentically also meant occasionally illustrating my preaching with stories of my own temptations or sins. But this authenticity can arise only from the relaxed confidence of knowing that I am accepted in Christ. We strive for Christlikeness *from* a position of acceptance, not *for* a position of acceptance.

This transparency is something we also want our children to develop. While we must maintain high standards, we also want them to live authentically. We do not want them to feel pressure to be "extra Christian" or "extra good" just because they are our children. Instead, we want them to develop their own inward walk with Jesus, seeking to live a life worthy of him for his sake, not ours. I tried to encourage this authenticity by telling my children that I would not be surprised by their questions about Christianity or sexuality. I had similar questions at their age, and this was a natural part of growing up. At other times, I reminded them that sin wanted to have them by themselves but that nothing would take away my love for them, so they didn't need to hide things from me.

11. C. H. Spurgeon, *The Metropolitain Tabernacle Pulpit* (London, 1875), 20:189.

Evidently the message got through. At a recent conference I conducted, I received the following question: "What would your kids say you did as a family that was most impactful for them in terms of their love for Christ?" I was speechless. I had no idea. I evaluate my parenting all the time by talking with them as adults. But I had never asked them this question. So, during the break, I quickly texted them. Their answers brought tears to my eyes, but one theme kept coming up. "You made it clear that what you thought mattered wasn't just the outward expressions or the rule-following but a real relationship with Jesus." Thank heavens they remember the good and have conveniently overlooked my sin!

One day, believe it or not, your young children will also be twenty-five, thirty-five, or forty-five. Will your love and authenticity be uppermost in their memory? Or will they feel that they had to be "perfect kids" for you or the church? Church leaders who are not afraid to be authentic give permission for others in the church to follow suit. You don't want to be a public success and a private failure.

CONCLUSION

Managing our households well involves more than having obedient, connected children. But not less. Children who are faithful to their parents and full of life display the gospel to the world. As men learn to exercise authoritative and affectionate leadership in the home, they are strengthening the same muscles that they will need in the church. Shepherding well is recognizing the sin nature of those in your care and taking proper initiative toward their obedience, all the while maintaining a warmhearted, fatherly love for them.

FOR REFLECTION AND APPLICATION

1. If you have young children, what is your initial reaction to the idea that you should "see that they obey you" or that you should "keep them submissive"?

2. If you have children, are you overseeing their training toward maturity and obedience? Or have you so delegated these duties to your wife that, functionally, you are not involved?
3. Good leadership involves both authority and affection. Which do you tend toward? What could you do to begin cultivating more of the other?
4. Think of good church leaders you know. How do they demonstrate both these qualities?
5. Would your wife and children say you are the same person in public that you are in private? Or do you feel the need to hide your sin? How did the section on authenticity challenge you?

3

FAITHFUL, NOT WILD

An elder must be blameless, the husband of one wife, with faithful children who are not accused of wildness or rebellion. (Titus 1:6 CSB)

A pastor wrote in to a well-known podcast,[1] asking the host a challenging question. From the time he was a teenager, all he wanted to do was pastor God's people. He had dedicated his life to this call. But he had recently had to resign as senior pastor of his church because his adult son had come out as bisexual and transgender and no longer considered himself to be his son. Based on Titus 1:6, he asked, was he disqualified for ministry?

Powerful, heartbreaking, emotional. But a question in need of our attention. Titus 1 is the second place in which Paul discusses the qualifications of an overseer. In this passage, home leadership heads the list of qualifications.

> An elder must be blameless, the husband of one wife, with faithful children who are not accused of wildness or rebellion.

1. Albert Mohler, host, *The Briefing*, podcast, May 10, 2024, 12:48, www.albert mohler.com/2024/05/10/briefing-5-10-24/.

> As an overseer of God's household, he must be blameless. (Titus 1:6–7 CSB)

God tells us that if an elder or a prospective elder has children, they must be "faithful children who are not accused of wildness or rebellion." Why? As we saw in 1 Timothy, and as we now see again in Titus, an elder is "an overseer of God's household." How he leads his smaller household demonstrates how he will lead God's household.

We will take our time as we walk through this qualification. Each word is important and has much to teach us. Titus 1:6 also has been misunderstood and misapplied, causing pain for many in the church. It often leads to questions like the one from the pastor mentioned above. For pastors' children, it can cause difficulties like those that Barnabas Piper records.[2] "Everyone's eyes are on you. All the time," says one pastor's kid. Another recalls, "I remember my mother telling me at a very young age that we were always being watched. That still stays with me until today." A better understanding of this passage in Titus might have alleviated some of the pain. To answer this need, the next two chapters will walk through how we are to understand and apply the Scripture.

CHILDREN

We will start with *children*. Believers have debated whether Paul is speaking about children who are still living in the home or offspring of any age. We have seen in 1 Timothy 3 that Paul wants us to draw inferences about a man's leadership skill, relational wisdom, and personal character by looking at how he carries out his duties as a father. Therefore, in Titus 1, we can conclude that Paul must also be considering how a father interacts with children who are still living in the household and under his direct influence.

2. Barnabas Piper, *The Pastor's Kid: Finding Your Own Faith and Identity* (David C Cook, 2014), 33.

John Stott concurs: "It is legitimate to ask for how long the faith and conduct of children remain their parents' responsibility. The text suggests that Paul has childhood in mind. For, although *tekna* ('children') could be used of posterity in general and occasionally of grown adults, it usually refers to youngsters who are still in their minority (which of course varies in different cultures) and are therefore regarded as being still under their parents' authority."[3]

Commentator George Knight agrees that Paul is speaking "only about children who are still rightfully under their father's authority in his home."[4] Thus, to understand this verse properly, we must start with a solid foundation. Paul is speaking about children who are in the household and under the direct relational influence of their father. Although we may look at an adult to gain insight into his or her father's character, there is not a *direct* connection between the two.

FAITHFUL . . . OR BELIEVING?

As we continue in this verse, we find a significant difference between modern English translations.

> An elder must be blameless, the husband of one wife, with faithful children who are not accused of wildness or rebellion. (CSB)

> . . . the husband of one wife, and his children are believers and not open to the charge of debauchery or insubordination. (ESV)

Did you catch it? Some translations—such as the ESV, the NIV, and the NASB—tell us that an elder must have *believing* children. Other

3. John Stott, *Guard the Truth: The Message of 1 Timothy & Titus* (InterVarsity Press, 1996), 176.

4. George W. Knight III, *The Pastoral Epistles,* The New International Greek Testament Commentary (Eerdmans, 1992), 289.

translations—such as the KJV, the CSB, and the NET—instruct us to look for *faithful* children. What did Paul mean? Why the difference? Is God really saying that for a man to be a leader in the church, all his children must follow Jesus Christ? We can all think of Christian leaders with wayward children who are nonetheless fruitfully serving the Lord.

The Greek word in question is *pistos*. It is translated as "believing" or "faithful" throughout the New Testament. For example, in 1 Timothy 6:2, it is typically translated as "believing," while in 2 Timothy 2:2, it is translated as "faithful" or "trustworthy." The correct translation depends on the context. Because translators know that either rendering of *pistos* could be possible in our passage from Titus 1, they usually indicate the alternative translation in a footnote at the bottom of the page in our English Bibles. Thus, those versions that translate *pistos* as "believing" include "faithful" at the bottom of the page, and vice versa. The translators are telling us, in essence, "Here is the translation we have chosen for this word, but the other one is also valid."[5]

FIVE REASONS TO PREFER *FAITHFUL* OVER *BELIEVING*

Properly understood, I believe "faithful" is the better translation. Here are five reasons why.

First, Scripture clearly teaches that salvation is a work of God. Our child's saving faith is by grace and not by works, neither ours nor theirs. No man has the ability to make his child believe the gospel. Every godly man whose children are walking with the Lord praises God, not himself. The purpose of this passage is to help us look for qualities in a man and his family for which he is responsible.

5. For a scholarly treatment of this subject, see Timothy E. Miller, "Unbelieving Child and Qualified Elder: A Case for 'Faithful' Children in Titus 1:6," *Themelios* 49, no. 2 (2024): 334–45, available online at www.thegospelcoalition.org/themelios/article/unbelieving-child-and-qualified-elder-a-case-for-faithful-children-in-titus-16/.

Second, Scripture must always interpret Scripture. In the parallel passage, 1 Timothy 3:4–5, Paul emphasizes that an elder must keep his children obedient or under control. Would Paul have given Titus a higher standard than Timothy? It's much more likely that Paul would have set the same standard using different words and a different emphasis. Studying Titus 1:6 deepens our understanding of 1 Timothy 3:4–5, and vice versa.

Third, "faithful" best matches the contrast. Paul tells us that a prospective leader's children are *not wild or rebellious*. If Paul had meant *believing* children, then we would expect to see the contrasting characteristic of *unbelieving*. Instead, Paul presents a contrast related to behavior—wildness and disobedience.

Fourth, misunderstanding this verse has led to painful consequences. To teach that the belief of his children is within an elder's control leads to a mechanistic understanding of salvation and false implications. The thinking goes, "A godly man will train up his children in the faith, and they will not depart from it. If they did depart as adults, there must be something deficient with the man. He must have done something wrong."[6] Too many fathers have borne this false guilt along with the heartbreak that comes with a prodigal. "What did I do wrong?" they think.

6. This understanding also comes from a misapplication of Proverbs 22:6. Historically, this verse has been understood to be a key text in considering family discipleship and a child's walk with God. However, there are two problems with making this a foundational verse for such purposes. First, this is a proverb and not a promise. It is the way things generally work, not the way they always work. Second, I would suggest that the primary application for this verse is a child's character training, not his or her salvation. You can read more at Chap Bettis, "Proverbs 22:6 – A Second Look at an Unpopular Verse," The Disciple-Making Parent, www.thedisciplemakingparent.com/proverbs-226-a-second-look-at-an-unpopular-verse/; and Chap Bettis, "Recovering Proverbs 22:6 for a New Generation," The Disciple-Making Parent, www.thedisciplemakingparent.com/recovering-proverbs-226-for-a-new-generation. See also Justin Taylor, "Unbelief in an Elder's Children," Desiring God, February 1, 2007, www.desiringgod.org/articles/unbelief-in-an-elders-children.

But this understanding is contradicted both by Scripture and by life. Salvation is by grace and not by works—not by the works of the child and *not by the works of the parents.* A godly parent speaks the gospel, shapes his children's will, and trains his children in the disciplines of the Christian faith, all the while praying for God to soften their hearts. Ordinarily, the good fruit of belief follows. But not always. There are just too many exceptions in which children who were raised in the same environment make very different choices.

Finally, numerous leaders concur with the translation. For example, George Knight believes that the word means "faithful" in the sense of being submissive or obedient, just as a servant or steward is regarded as faithful when he carries out the requests of his master (see Matt. 24:45–47; 25:21, 23).[7] Knight points to extrabiblical evidence that indicates that the word means "faithful." Alexander Strauch also concurs with this view:

> The parallel passage in 1 Timothy 3:4 states that the prospective elder must keep "his children under control with all dignity." Since 1 Timothy 3:4 is the clearer passage, it should be allowed to help interpret the ambiguity of Titus 1:6. "Under control with all dignity" is closely parallel with "having trustworthy children." In the Titus passage, however, the qualification is stated in a positive form—the elder must have children who are trustworthy and dutiful.
>
> Those who interpret this qualification to mean that an elder must have believing, Christian children place an impossible burden upon a father.[8]

7. Knight, *Pastoral Epistles,* 290, mentions a deed of sale in which a slave is described as "faithful and not given to running away." Knight also mentions an epitaph for a slave that reads "I remain faithful as before."

8. Alexander Strauch, *Biblical Eldership: An Urgent Call to Restore Biblical Church Leadership,* rev. ed. (Lewis and Roth, 1995), 229.

FAITHFUL CHILDREN

If we understand this passage to mean *faithful* children living in the home, what exactly does this entail? We have just seen that it involves being under the control of their father rather than running wild. This directly matches the parallel found in 1 Timothy 3:4. The children submit to and obey their father.

But the language of "faithful children" conveys a richer idea than mere white-knuckle obedience. Faithfulness carries the idea of steadfastness in affection or allegiance. Faithful children love their father. They listen to their father's counsel and respect his values. These children trust their father and thus obey him. In other words, the father of faithful children lives in a way that it makes it natural for his children to believe in him. He engenders a relationship that inspires respect and love.[9] Even in the teen years, we would expect to see a sense of affection for Mom and Dad. A surly or isolated teen tells us that the relationship is broken.

Of course, such an expression of faithfulness will be tested by outside circumstances and the development of a child. As young children mature into teens, other factors will challenge their relationship. But a wise father will do all he can to maintain his children's trust. He will have the relational wisdom to make adjustments and to respond well. Perhaps a fourteen-year-old son is pulling away from the family and becoming more absorbed in the gaming world. This could lead to a mere clash of wills if Dad comes at his son with anger and demands. Or it could be an opportunity to come alongside the teen and inquire about what's captivating him in the online world. It could be a chance for the father to calmly set limits and explain his deeper concerns. Even amid conflict, this father is integrating authority with affection. We are looking for a man who raises children connected to his heart.

9. "The glory of children is their fathers" (Prov. 17:6). There is a natural love and respect in this relationship unless it is destroyed.

FAITHFULNESS TO THE GOSPEL

When a loving father teaches his children the gospel, and when they trust their father, then we could expect them to embrace his God. This brings us full circle. Even as we remove the unbiblical expectation that all an elder's children must be believers, we can still expect that, barring exceptional circumstances, most children in his home will profess Christ as their Savior. This is a gracious outworking of hearing the sweet news of the gospel from a source they trust.

I am not at all discounting the need for the Holy Spirit to regenerate the heart. This supernatural work absolutely must happen. Nor am I dismissing the absolute necessity of other saints in helping us evangelize and disciple our children. I am merely restating the general heart direction of one who grows up in a Christian home. She becomes one of the faithful by staying faithful to the good teaching of her church and her parents.

Children born into believing households, with believing fathers, are uniquely blessed. Even though a father cannot personally give his children new life, God does work through means. From a young age, children in believing families have the opportunity to hear the gospel tenderly preached and lived. Fathers have a special responsibility to hold out the gospel to their children, teach them to love Jesus, and train them in the disciplines of the faith, trusting that they may receive it in due time.

While we don't want to pressure a child to profess faith, we must also not neglect to speak the gospel. We cannot think that a man has *no* influence on his child's faith. He does! Let's not be careless as we evangelize and disciple our children. We want to do all we can to lead them to the Savior.

A godly man should so diligently oversee his household that the children under his direct influence desire to profess the faith of their fathers. Knowing that loving the Lord is a godly parenting goal, an intentional father will teach his children obedience while also monitoring their heart attitudes. He will not be satisfied with mere outward compliance from his child but will say, "Give me your heart, *and* give your heart to Jesus." In short, we are looking for a man who has raised his children to be faithful toward himself and God.

NOT WILD OR REBELLIOUS

Finally, God instructs us that an elder's children must not be *wild or rebellious*. They should not live in rebellion against God's standards and their father's standards. This looks different for a six-year-old than a sixteen-year-old. For example, a six-year-old may ignore his father's commands and run the other way when called. When a sixteen-year-old is habitually unfaithful, he is unruly and alienated. He is, simply put, out of control (see 1 Tim. 3:4 CSB).

The word translated as "wild," *asótia*, is also used of the Prodigal Son. It describes an individual who is indulging in the wasteful vices of the unbelieving world, and it would more accurately be used of a teen than of a young child. "Rebellious," on the other hand, is a translation of the word *anupotaktos*, which means undisciplined, disobedient, or unruly.[10] It could be used of young children as well as teens.

Why is having wild and disobedient children a black mark on a father? Because these children are still in his home, and their wild behavior demonstrates that he has not been properly interacting with them. Paul is not speaking of children who are occasionally wild or disobedient but rather of those who are characterized by rebellion against their parents. And why are the children characterized by this? Because their parents—and particularly their fathers—have not implemented appropriate negative consequences for their misbehavior. Parenting is always a dynamic interaction in the context of a relationship. Actions that are in line with God's Word bring about positive consequences, while sinful actions bring about negative consequences.

This interaction will constantly change as children grow older and encounter different temptations. Compliant children

10. Knight, *Pastoral Epistles*, 290.

may suddenly become challenging teenagers. Friends may pull their hearts away. As parents, we must not be surprised when the rebellion within our children's hearts suddenly rises to the surface. Having raised four teenagers, Sharon and I certainly had our trying moments. We did not always handle these trials well. There were times when sin came out and we had to put consequences in place. In a loving home, where the parents are comfortable exercising their God-appointed authority, parents react to disobedience with love. This will likely entail intimate conversations through which parents can draw near to a heart that has grown distant. But it might also include consequences that cause a six- or sixteen-year-old to realize the nature of his or her actions. Perhaps, out of wisdom, it just involves observation with no comment or imposed consequence. Jonathan Leeman helpfully observes, "It takes skill and wisdom to simultaneously lead people in the right direction while letting them figure out their direction on their own."[11] A wise father thinks this way regarding his teenage children.

Does a suddenly rebellious child cast doubt on the character of the father? No, Paul is referring to situations in which children have become wild or disobedient and *the father does nothing about it*. His permissiveness and passivity are character flaws that are unfitting in a leader of a biological family or of God's family. We will think about how to handle family trials in the next chapter.

CONCLUSION

A godly father loves the Lord and his children. While they are in his home, such a father will lead his children to be faithful to him and his Savior. He will actively teach them the Scriptures. He will skillfully shepherd them through challenges and watch over their hearts. Though he cannot control what they do after they leave his

11. Jonathan Leeman, *Authority: How Godly Rule Protects the Vulnerable, Strengthens Communities, and Promotes Human Flourishing* (Crossway, 2023), 21.

household, he has shown his skill as a dad and a pastor. This is the kind of man we want shepherding the church.

How would I have responded to the pastor whose question began this chapter? Though he gives us very little information, I might have said, "Brother, my heart goes out to you. I can think of no pain greater than to have your son reject you and the God who loves him. Having an adult child who is rebellious does not necessarily disqualify you from ministry. However, as pastors, we do represent the Lord and his righteousness. Some adult behavior is rebellion born out of an individual's foolish choices. But other decisions can be made in reaction to hidden sins in the family that are just now coming to light. To gain clarity, invite your leadership team—or another group of trusted, mature men—to interview your son and your wife. Godly men will know the difference between the indwelling sin that we all have and a sin that has exasperated a child. If you do step down, it should be for your character issues that have come to light, not for the lifestyle your son has chosen. If you were faithful to teach him the gospel and love him, albeit imperfectly, then no reproach falls on you."

FOR REFLECTION AND APPLICATION

1. Have you studied Titus 1:6 before? Does the explanation presented in this chapter differ from your prior understanding? If so, how?
2. Without demanding that all an elder's children believe, we have considered the idea of faithfulness to the father and the father's God. What did you think of this idea?
3. If you have children, what are you doing to capture their hearts?
4. What are you doing to lead your children to the Savior and train them in the gospel disciplines?
5. Do you see preaching the gospel and training the character as two different things? How are they different? How are they similar?

4

ABOVE REPROACH

In this world you will have trouble. But take heart! I have overcome the world. (John 16:33 NIV)

I'm staring at a family photo taken at the recent wedding of my oldest. In it, my adult children and their spouses are dressed formally and smiling. It is a wonderful moment of perfection captured in time. But it is just that—a moment of us at our best. It does not reflect what we all know to be true: Family life is messy.

Whenever I ask men, "Do you manage your household well?" I hear answers like "I don't know" or "I hope so." Why this disconnect between what Scripture clearly prescribes and our own understanding? I think the answers to my question can be vague because we know how messy our families are. Perhaps you are just recovering from a disagreement with your wife. Or maybe one of your children is acting out, and you don't know what to do. You think your family should always look like that smiling, formal wedding portrait.

But sometimes our insecurity comes from more than that. Maybe *church* members think our families should always look like that wedding portrait. Or, to change the metaphor, that our families should never go through any storms. A well-managed home, the thinking goes, never experiences any disturbances. It is all smooth sailing and happily ever after.

Nothing could be further from the truth. As our good friend Spurgeon states with a twinkle in his eye, "There are difficulties in everything except in eating pancakes."[1] In this chapter we will take a look at two different but related topics. First, does going through a family storm mean that a ministry leader should step down from his position? Second, what does it mean to *lead well* through the inevitable storms that will come our way?

WHAT IS "ABOVE REPROACH"?

Let's start with the common misconception that church leaders must have picture-perfect families. Where has this idea come from? The answer, I believe, is that it arises from a misunderstanding of the qualities of an elder. In both 1 Timothy 3 and Titus 1, Paul begins his list of qualifications with an overarching quality. Overseers, he says, are to be "above reproach." Reproach refers to anything upon which an adversary could base a charge. Jeramie Rinne states in his book on elders, "A man who is above reproach displays an exemplary degree of Christlikeness, free from conspicuous sin."[2]

Rather than this definition, many have taken *above reproach* to mean perfect and without problems. It is one thing to desire exemplary leaders, but it is quite another to expect them to be flawless. This error is doubly compounded when we apply this mis-qualification to a leader's family. As one man said to me, "Shouldn't an elder's family be a model family?" The answer to this question is yes . . . and no. If by "model family" you mean one that presents a shiny, problem-free facade to everyone, then the answer is no. That type of family may be modeling something, but it is not displaying authenticity and its need for grace—in other words, the gospel.

1. C. H. Spurgeon, *John Ploughman's Pictures* (Springfield, OH, 1881), 78.
2. Jeramie Rinne, *Church Elders: How to Shepherd God's People Like Jesus* (Crossway, 2014), 21.

However, if by "model family" you mean one in which a man is modeling how one sinner leads other sinners to Jesus, how he initiates care for his wife and children, how he disciplines his children *and* allows them to grow into their own people, then, yes, they are to be a model family. Our exemplary husband loves his wife through the inevitable ups and downs that come when two sinners marry. He confesses his sin to her when he errs and seeks her forgiveness. Our model dad is neither permissive nor perfectionistic. His goal is not to raise children who make him look good or to prevent criticism. In fact, he is not raising children at all, but adults. He's in it for the long haul, seeking their hearts when they are twenty-five.

Some Christians have held the erroneous idea that having problems automatically disqualifies a man from spiritual leadership. This belief springs from the incorrect assumption that if you do everything right, you will escape problems. This is simply not true. What did Jesus do wrong that caused all the disciples to deny him and one to betray him? The answer, of course, is that Jesus didn't do anything wrong. While poor leadership can cause problems, good leadership does not eliminate them.

Managing well does not mean that we never encounter problems. It means that we handle problems well. The sin that our key passages address is not the problems themselves but the lack of response to the problems. The black mark on Eli and David was that they knew the evil their children were doing and yet *did nothing about it* (1 Sam. 3:13; 1 Kings 1:6). They were passive and permissive.

Family life is messy. Shepherding God's people in the church is also messy. There is always some new challenge facing us. Caring for a family involves a constant struggle to bring order out of chaos. A well-managed family is more like a well-cared-for flock of sheep than a finely tuned engine. The latter can run nicely with relatively little attention. The former needs constant watchfulness, adjustment, protection, and care. In a well-managed flock, there will always be straying or stubborn sheep.

PASTORAL IMPLICATIONS FOR THE UNPAID ELDER OR DEACON

So how are we to think about times when a leader is going through a storm? At the risk of oversimplifying, let me make some pastoral suggestions for handling different situations that may occur. I offer these knowing that each church situation and family situation is unique. However, I believe there are two different scenarios we need to consider: the unpaid leader and the paid leader.

Let's start by thinking of the man who is already serving as an unpaid elder or deacon when a storm comes upon his family. Perhaps a faithful and compliant child suddenly closes off his heart. My associate pastor, Travis, is a perfect example of this.

When Travis was in ninth grade, a close friend of his died in a car accident. Even though he had been raised in a godly home, Travis deliberately decided to turn away from the Lord. "God," he said, "if this is what you are going to do to me, I will run from you. I will try and break all your commandments." He dove headfirst into rebellion and drug use, bringing chaos into the home. His father, a deacon, responded to this new rebellion with appropriate consequences. By Travis's own testimony, it was a tumultuous time, but *it was not due to his father*. In fact, his father and mother were meeting these new challenges with engagement, consequences, rules, and conversation.

While his father took time to step back from his diaconal duties to devote more time to the chaos at home, his son's rebellion did not mean that he should not have been an officer. In fact, the strength of his father's character became increasingly apparent as he navigated this storm.

The teen years seem to present special challenges for many parents. As I talk with those who have grown up in Christian homes, many recount times of testing and rebellion. "Did your parents do anything to cause that?" I have often asked. The responses are very similar: "No, I just wanted to live a life apart from Christ." Nothing had changed in the father's character. The sinful hearts of children had brought this storm on the whole family.

These trials don't come only from children. Another lay elder shared with me the problems he was having in his marriage. Seemingly without warning, his wife had become contentious. She was opposing him and tearing him down in private. As he said to me, "Her heart is outside my control." But this good brother handled the storm well. He got individuals in the church involved. He listened, prayed, and listened some more. He confessed his own sin when appropriate. He encouraged her to get counseling, which eventually resolved the issue. In other words, he was not passive amid the trial. He took the initiative to actively care for his wife and his marriage.

No doubt there are many more examples we could list. In each of these cases, the leaders did not step down from their position, but they did spend extra time and give more attention at home. They also brought the other leaders of the church into their lives and shared the storm with them. In those discussions, they offered to step down if the other leaders thought they should.

In another instance, a man with young children had been installed as an elder. As his children grew, it became obvious that he and his wife did not have the same parenting philosophy, which was evidenced by the lack of correction of his children. He stepped down as a lay elder until they could get on the same page. Similarly, no man can serve as a church leader without the support of his wife. The demands are just too great. If she is not unified with him in this calling, then maybe he should not be leading in the church.

THE PAID PASTOR

For the paid pastor, the situation is a little bit different. Congregations often have a higher standard for one who receives a salary from the church. We need to revisit the criteria we have already mentioned in chapter 3 and above. Managing well does not mean having a perfect family. It means being a dad who isn't permissive and passive or harsh and domineering.

Assuming he has been an engaged dad, then a storm like a child's rebellion does not change anything about a man's qualification to serve. In fact, if anything, we want to draw close and study his example as he walks through the issue. A man's character is revealed in a trial. The problem gives the leadership team a chance to come alongside this brother. It is an opportunity for greater transparency and greater support. The paid pastor might be given more family time so that he can walk through the issues at home. Rather than abandoning the leader, the church should take the opportunity to pray for his family. Doing so reminds us that there is only one Savior and Shepherd; the rest of us are merely flawed undershepherds.

A church needs to affirm its understanding of 1 Timothy 3 and Titus 1 even before a storm hits. Knowing that he will not be fired for facing storms will encourage a pastor to be more transparent about his family life. And it will also minister indirectly to the pastor's children. Barnabas Piper describes the burden older pastor's children often feel: "The pressure of keeping my father in his job by being 'submissive' is not something that makes me (or any other PK [pastor's kid]) want to follow Jesus. The tacit reminder that our rebellion may cost Dad his job is not an expression of grace leading to repentance and restoration. It is a cause for resentment."[3]

Asking a man to step down because of poor decisions made by his child only increases the complexity of the problem. If he is forced to resign, he must look for another job and will have even less time to shepherd the troubled teen. The family now has two crises to deal with, not one! Moreover, the rebellious teenage child is watching the church abandon his father because of him. He has caused his father to lose his job! This will further solidify his opposition to Christianity.

This counsel needs to be balanced by my comments at the end of the last chapter. As elders, we do represent the Lord and his righteousness. When we hit storms, we should open our lives to other wise men

3. Barnabas Piper, *The Pastor's Kid: Finding Your Own Faith and Identity* (David C Cook, 2014), 76.

who can speak into our situation. I know of several paid pastors who, each upon realizing he had a recalcitrant prodigal, brought it to the attention of his leadership team. The team weighed their knowledge of the Scriptures, the man, and the child. Eventually, in these cases, they encouraged the pastors to continue in ministry. These pastors with prodigals did so knowing that they had humbled themselves before others.

GOD'S WORK IN THE LEADER

No family storm is ever enjoyable. I weathered several over the years of raising four children. I made plenty of mistakes and would never have chosen to go through them. Looking back, however, I am glad the Lord sent them. In fact, this might be the foundational truth you need to remember as you are going through those trials: The Lord is in the midst of the storm with you, and he has sent it for your good.

Some have said that heartaches make for better pastors. "Perhaps the greatest qualifications, the best instruction, the most useful learning, that any Christian minister can attain, without any disparagement of other kinds of learning, is that which is attained in the school of affliction; it is by this he becomes able to feel, to sympathize, and to speak a word in season to them that are weary."[4] I can testify from personal experience that individual and family trials have led me to cry out to the Lord more. They have softened my hard edges and given me more compassion for others.

4. Andrew Fuller, *The Complete Works of Andrew Fuller*, vol. 1, *The Diary of Andrew Fuller, 1780–1801*, ed. Michael D. McMullen and Timothy D. Whelan (De Gruyter, 2016), 390–91, as quoted in Collin Hansen and Jeff Robinson, eds., *12 Faithful Men: Portraits of Courageous Endurance in Pastoral Ministry* (Baker, 2018), 99.

LEADING WELL IN THE STORM

Understanding that trials will come, how does a leader respond in a godly manner? Let me suggest at least three steps in the process of handling storms well.

First, we seek to lessen problems. Rather than being a reactive leader, a wise father and pastor tries to think ahead. Some problems arise because leaders are reactive and not proactive.

Just as a regular oil change keeps a car's engine healthy, so do some actions "oil" the natural frictions of life. Whether I am leading my family or my church, there are rhythms I can establish that will foster everyone's health. For example, as a pastor, I might schedule a regular marriage or parenting conference. I do this not because of any specific problems but because I know the nature of sin and the need for regular training in the home.

For parents, this might mean making sure that our children aren't out too late so that we don't have issues the next day. It might mean connecting to the heart during the tweenage years because you know that there will be bumps when they become teenagers. A wise person looks down the road. As a leader, I want to avoid exasperating the people under my care. However, even careful preparation will not eliminate all problems. And that brings us to the next principle.

Second, we lean into the problems. If I am not expecting family life or leadership to be problem free, then I will not be surprised when trials arise. I can recognize that these issues have come from the Lord's hand to sanctify and mature me. One reason a church or a family has leaders is to guide them through the inevitable rough times. By way of analogy, we see the true skills of a pilot not when the weather is smooth but when it is stormy.

Leaning into a problem means that I should not ignore an issue, hoping it will go away. I must learn to move toward hard conversations. I must not try to hide the messiness of my family. I believe it is God's grace when he allows secret sin to be exposed. I must make sure that I am responding appropriately—not harshly overreacting or passively underreacting. I must learn to discern what is important and what is not. I must ask others for help as needed. Leaning in means moving toward the problem even if I don't know what to do. I must realize that I am in a providential storm, one that the Lord has allowed for my good and his glory. And he has put me in the pilot's seat.

Understanding my role to pilot through the storm also reminds me of how important my own steadiness is. My calmness and faith minister to others. After facing her own crisis, a friend's teenage daughter said to him, "Dad, everything is OK because you are here." As family and church shepherds, we have a ministry of presence during hard times. The shepherd's faith and peace can calm the sheep.

But handling conflict in the moment is not where I stop. What happens after the crisis is over?

Third, we learn from problems. As the old adage goes, "Fool me once, shame on you. Fool me twice, shame on me." The point? That we should learn from our mistakes. A wise leader will analyze the problem and think about ways to prepare for, and even prevent, the reoccurrence of that problem. In other words, a smart shepherd has the self-awareness to ask, "Why did we get into this mess? What can I do differently next time? How could this be prevented?" A maturing leader is constantly learning lessons about himself and about others. He is developing convictions about overseeing others that can mitigate problems. Families and churches will all have issues and conflicts. But wise leaders will navigate with a steady hand through the storm and learn lessons for next time.

Managing your households well does not mean that you have no problems, but it does mean that you handle problems well.

CONCLUSION

You will have trials in your family and in your church. There may be an occasion when the secret sin of a child comes out. Or perhaps you have an older child who declares that he is not a Christian or wants to live an alternate lifestyle. The issue may be a stormy time in your marriage due to circumstances outside your control. You may feel shame, guilt, or confusion. But God has not left you. The question is this: "How will you lead well now?"

FOR REFLECTION AND APPLICATION

1. Have you ever thought that "above reproach" meant a leader's home should not have problems? In what ways may you have unconsciously communicated that wrong idea to your family? To other leaders?
2. Are you in the midst of a parenting or marriage storm now? Have you shared appropriate details with others? Who?
3. Do men in your church feel free to share difficulties in their homes with one another? Or does everyone just assume that things are going fine? How could sharing some of your past trials encourage others?
4. If you are a leader, does your church believe that any storm requires you to step down? Or does your church hold the position for leaders suggested in this chapter? Have you discussed it with others in positions of authority?
5. We noted three suggestions for leading well in a storm: (1) Seek to lessen problems. (2) Lean into problems. (3) Learn from problems. Which one seems hardest to you? Why?

PART 2

LEADERSHIP LESSONS FOR HOME AND CHURCH

5

LEARNING TO LEAD AND OVERSEE

When one rules justly over men, ruling in the fear of God, he dawns on them like the morning light, like the sun shining forth on a cloudless morning, like rain that makes grass to sprout from the earth. (2 Sam. 23:3–4)

I was having lunch with a friend and church member. As we were talking about his family, he confessed, "It's easier to lead my twenty-five-million-dollar company than to lead my wife and three girls." My friend was just articulating what we all know. Leadership in the home is difficult. Business leaders have paychecks at their disposal. They can ask employees to work overtime, knowing they need the money. Job descriptions and tasks are usually much simpler than the complexities of nurturing a family. Goals and accomplishments are often much clearer.

Leadership in the home is different. Unlike shallow workplace relationships, family relationships are deeply personal. While managers may call their team a family, our families really are . . . our families. The challenges in a family are often emotionally charged. The goals and outcomes are often less obvious. A business may measure success by its profits and the number of sales, but how do you measure success in a family? Maybe that's why so many men don't know if they are leading their families well. What are the markers?

In the first section of this book, we discussed the biblical teaching that a man can and should manage his home well. God would not have given pastors and deacons a requirement that they cannot meet by the power of the Spirit. We looked at the specific application Paul makes—is a man overseeing obedient children who are connected to his heart? Has he mastered authority and affection? Paul cares about these qualities because our homes display whether or not we have the relational wisdom to care for God's church.

But leading your household well is not limited to having obedient children. This one objective does not exhaust how a man can oversee his family well. Your marriage and other parts of your household also display and develop your leadership skills. In this second section of the book, we will focus specifically on areas of oversight in the home that can carry over to the church. Learning these lessons will make you a more skilled shepherd of God's household.

In this chapter, we will look at how a man can develop leadership skills in his home. Then we will think about family management, or oversight skills. Third, we will examine developing and deploying others. Finally, we will discuss why a leader must have patience and persistence.

LEARNING TO LEAD

But the noble man makes noble plans, and by noble deeds he stands.
(Isa. 32:8 NIV)

"How can I lead when I don't know where I am going?" an earnest new husband asked me. I understood his confusion and distress. For something that is talked about so much, we can be unclear on what leadership in the home actually *is*. When this young husband asked me the question, he was thinking about where his family will live in five years or what he will do for work. He didn't know the answers to those questions. As a result, he felt stymied. His misunderstanding of family leadership is all too common.

Let's start by making sure we understand what leadership is. John Piper's definition has been helpful for me: "Spiritual leadership [is] knowing where God wants people to be and taking the initiative to use God's methods to get them there in reliance on God's power."[1] Spiritual leadership in the home is knowing where God wants your family to be and taking the initiative to get them there.[2] While you may not know where you will live in five years, there are a number of things that you *do* know God desires.

We know that Christ desires us to build strong marriages in which we are emotionally connected to and communicating with our spouses (see Eph. 5:25). His Spirit will give us the strength to pursue this goal. We do not want to have weak or conflict-ridden marriages. We also understand that God wants our children to grow into young adults who love Jesus Christ, provide for themselves, and join a healthy local church. Again, Jesus promises his empowering presence as we seek to disciple our children toward these objectives (see Matt. 28:19–20). A godly man understands these goals and will take practical measures to see that his family moves toward them.

For example, to help accomplish the goal of having a healthy marriage, you and your wife may make plans to get away on your anniversary. To move toward the objective of having obedient children, you might ensure that both of you have an agreed-upon plan for training the children. To build a strong family identity, you may initiate memorable vacations. Or to help shepherd your children to maturity, you'll likely have hard conversations with them. In all this, you will need to take the initiative to build a strong family. You will also need to make adjustments in light of the inevitable challenges that arise throughout that journey.

This is what a growing leader does. He believes that Jesus himself is taking the initiative to build his church through him (see Matt. 16:18). The Lord raises up shepherds for the progress and joy of

1. John Piper, "The Marks of a Spiritual Leader," Desiring God, January 1, 1995, www.desiringgod.org/articles/the-marks-of-a-spiritual-leader.

2. See appendix A for a more detailed exploration of this aspect of leadership.

the saints (see Phil. 1:25). Therefore, a wise leader starts with a set of convictions regarding what makes a strong family or a family of God. He also has an awareness of the needs and maturity levels of individual family members. Finally, he makes plans for the group to move toward where he believes God wants them. In the area of sports, this was the problem with Will, our basketball coach from the introduction. He had no vision of a strong basketball team, nor was he tuned into the challenges his team was facing. As a result, he did not encourage them or make necessary changes.

While we always ought to be watchful and deliberate, taking the initiative does not mean we do everything. Sometimes we will need to delegate to others (more about this in a few pages). At other times, we may need to let our children struggle. We do this not because we are passive and clueless but because we know that the struggle is maturing them. Those prone to helicopter parenting might view this as "neglect," but it is actually a purposeful stepping back.

Whether leading his family, a small group, a ministry team, or an entire church, a good leader knows what a healthy group looks like, evaluates where things currently stand, and takes the initiative to strengthen those he is leading. This is the essence of skillful leadership. A family gives you a perfect chance to develop and display these abilities.

Leading your little household well will display that you can lead God's larger household well.

LEARNING TO MANAGE

He must manage his own household well, with all dignity keeping his children submissive. (1 Tim. 3:4)

Let deacons each be the husband of one wife, managing their children and their own households well. (1 Tim. 3:12)

"I preach and cast vision. I don't get involved in the details." That was the response of one pastor to me regarding how he understood his calling. No wonder several ministry leaders serving underneath him had quietly complained to me about the lack of encouragement and direction in his leadership. The problem? The pastor had no vision for the biblical calling of oversight or managing. The ministry heads underneath him were floundering without direction.

Leading any group of people, whether it be our families or a ministry team or the church, will require some oversight—that is, management. A leader-manager brings people together with the right structure and training to achieve common goals. This answers the "how are we going to get there" of leadership.[3]

We see this oversight clearly in the life of Nehemiah. As a leader, he surveyed the need, cast the vision, and inspired others. As a manager, he delegated specific work to specific individuals. He ensured that the plans were executed and that the goals were met. He encouraged his men in their work, making sure that they had all the supplies they needed. When discouragement, conflict, and opposition inevitably arose, he addressed those issues. Without Nehemiah's leadership *and* management, the wall would never have been built. Likewise, Jesus's development of the disciples and Paul's oversight of his apostolic team involved these same skills. Whenever there is a group of people moving toward a goal, there must be management.

How does this apply to you as a husband and a dad? Let me illustrate. My children had a set of grandparents who lived in the South, but I had stayed in New England to plant and pastor a church. Since we wanted our children to love their grandparents (a leadership goal), we resolved to make a yearly trip to Alabama (a leadership strategy). When our third child turned two, this meant no more airplane trips. As a pastor, I could not afford five tickets. Instead, we loaded everyone into our minivan for the two-day trip to the

3. See Albert Mohler, "Leaders Are Managers," chap. 14 in *The Conviction to Lead: 25 Principles for Leadership That Matters* (Bethany House, 2012), for further development of this idea. As he states, "management is leadership put into action" (118).

South. With four children in a minivan for twenty-two hours, Sharon and I had to think creatively about their activities and their limits. And all this was in the day before DVD players and personal video games! It was exhausting and rewarding. At times we were casting vision. "We are almost to the hotel and the pool!" or "Almost to Mimi's house. It's going to be great!" And other times we were managing—overseeing their play, deciding when to stop and eat, refereeing the squabbles, and, yes, knowing when they had hit their limits. Thus, the leadership of taking the initiative to keep children and grandparents connected required us to manage the trip. And was it worth it? Absolutely! My adult children look back fondly on the twelve trips we took down and back, and they have a great relationship with their grandparents.

As a dad, you need to look over your whole family and be aware of how they are doing. You will want to regularly talk with your wife to make sure that she has everything she needs to succeed. Sometimes overseeing well means stepping in when there is discouragement or disunity in your family. You will also want to take care that you are not overcommitted, a constant danger for families in our day. Managing may mean delegating chores to our children and holding them responsible for their execution. It will mean monitoring the atmosphere in our homes even as we disciple our families to love and follow Jesus Christ.

As you oversee in the church, you will need to employ the same kind of management skill. You want to develop the members of your team, put them in their place of giftedness, and clearly communicate the vision to the whole team. You'll need to look for bottlenecks that prevent people from fulfilling their jobs. You should facilitate training that will allow people to be successful. You will delegate and oversee. A wise manager doesn't do all the work, but he stays connected to those who are involved.

Managing or overseeing your little household well helps teach you the skills needed to oversee God's household well.

LEARNING TO DEVELOP AND DEPLOY THOSE ON YOUR TEAM

Then the Lord God said, "It is not good that the man should be alone; I will make him a helper fit for him." (Gen. 2:18)

Implied in our last section was the need to develop and deploy those on your team. Teamwork is crucial to success in ministry. We are not meant to serve alone. Yet leaders who can easily influence a crowd often find it difficult to lead a team. Their initiative can be unclear or nonexistent. While the public ministry is flourishing, the team might be dysfunctional.

Even a cursory study of Jesus's ministry shows that while he taught the crowds, he was also training his disciples. He was developing a team to continue and expand the ministry long after he was gone. He continues that work through godly shepherds today.

If you are a pastor, Ephesians 4:12 makes clear that part of your job is to equip the saints for the work of ministry. In other words, individuals in the body of Christ are the true Christian ministers. Wise Christian leaders will learn how to recruit, train, and encourage others on their team.

Where can we grow in this skill? In our homes!

In some ways, this crucial section gives a proper perspective to the whole book. God calls a man to oversee his household well. But he also calls us to provide for our families. Supporting our families financially involves hard work in a thorn-filled world. Those who have secular jobs will often need to work long hours. Pastoring, whether financially supported or not, is deeply labor-intensive.

How do we both provide for our families and manage well? We delegate to and partner with the one who is our greatest teammate! Even as this book is calling men to engage and oversee their households, we must realize that our wives are also called to join us in this task. A survey of numerous Scripture passages reveals the important roles that our wives play as life-givers and disciple-makers.[4] God's call for men to lead in the home is a call for us to appreciate our wives' own gifts. It is a call to delegate. For men, there are two common errors we need to avoid. On the one hand, a husband and father can be passive in his oversight. Rather than actively delegate, he can essentially abdicate his leadership role. On the other hand, a man can be overbearing, micromanaging, and controlling. We need to avoid both sinful extremes.

As your greatest teammate, your wife will either double your ministry effectiveness or halve it. It took me years to think of Sharon as a teammate to be developed and deployed. I learned to make sure that she had everything she needed to be successful, including a clear and biblical plan for parenting. As a team leader, I wanted to develop and encourage her in how she served our family and the Lord. We took this teamwork so seriously that she and I would go out on regular coffee dates just to talk about how we were doing and what was next for our family. We were working together as a unit to build a life, a family, and a ministry that honored the Lord.

J. Oswald Sanders, speaking of the need for leaders to learn the art of delegation, wrote, "One facet of leadership is the ability to recognize the special abilities and limitations of others, combined with the capacity to fit each one into the job where he or she will do best. To succeed in getting things done through others is the highest type of leadership."[5]

We as pastors have a unique perspective on our congregants' strengths and on opportunities to serve in the church. We bless others by recognizing and affirming strengths in them and then connecting them to a need within the church. We want to notice how God has gifted people and then have them use those gifts. This is one way pastors equip their flocks for service.

Yet learning to delegate and motivate is difficult. And it is even more difficult in an organization composed mostly of volunteers,

4. See Genesis 2:18; 3:16, 20; Proverbs 31:10–31; 1 Timothy 5:14; Titus 2:4.
5. J. Oswald Sanders, *Spiritual Leadership*, 2nd ed. (Moody, 1994), 137.

such as the church. Managers in the business world can learn some transferable skills. But church leaders must grasp these skills as well. I certainly learned some hard lessons as I pastored. How much better to begin mastering delegation skills in the home!

You are leading God's household well as you learn to develop and deploy those on your team.

LEARNING PATIENCE *AND* PERSISTENCE

As a father shows compassion to his children, so the Lord shows compassion to those who fear him. For he knows our frame; he remembers that we are dust. (Ps. 103:13–14)

All this talk about leading and delegating leaves out two important qualities—patience and persistence. Like the Christian life in general, both pastoring well and parenting well require what Eugene Peterson called "a long obedience in the same direction."[6] Yet, what do younger leaders often lack? Both patience and persistence.

Our children give us a perfect chance to grow in Christlike patience. They challenge us when we are most exhausted. They expose our idols of order, control, and progress. They are little sanctification machines that shine a floodlight on ways we need to grow. In all this we have opportunities to be transformed, to grow in forbearance like our heavenly Father. When we tie one more shoe, answer one more question, pick up one more piece of clothing, have one more late-night conversation, we are developing patience. We must remember that love *is* patient (see 1 Cor. 13:4).

Patience alone, however, is not enough. We need patient persistence for our children's progress (see Phil. 1:25). Fathers are to *bring up* their children. Children will not bring up themselves (see Prov. 29:15). Godly parenting is endurance with a goal. We want

6. See Eugene H. Peterson, *A Long Obedience in the Same Direction: Discipleship in an Instant Society* (InterVarsity Press, 2000).

our children to grow up to love and follow Jesus, but this long-term objective will require patient persistence toward that end. We see both those qualities in Jesus's ministry to his disciples. He taught and retaught his followers. He bore with their misunderstandings and arguments. And he continues to bear with us as we grow in Christlikeness over time. However, his patience has a purpose: to train us to be mature disciples.

Leaders often face temptation in both these areas. Some are impatient with the rate of individual or corporate growth. That was my temptation. As a young church planter, I wanted our church to grow—and now! Today, I can see so much pride in my own life that God had to work on. Other leaders are tempted to passively let their churches drift. Whether from discouragement or cynicism, these leaders are not taking the initiative to help the church progress in godliness. They just oversee directionless activity. If the church isn't helping others make progress toward Christlikeness, then it becomes like a cruise ship traveling in circles.

Mark Dever regularly reminds young men, "Pastors often overestimate what they can do in one year and underestimate what they can do in twenty." In your leadership role, are you both patient and persistent? Are you understanding of those you lead and crystal clear on where you are leading them? Your family gives you a chance to grow in all these qualities.

You are managing your households well if you are becoming more patient over time *and* more clear on where you are going.

CONCLUSION

You may not be the CEO of a corporation like my friend, but if you are a husband or a father, God calls you to lead well. Your little household provides a number of opportunities to grow in your leadership skills. You can take practical steps to help your little flock become stronger. You can also learn to be a watchful overseer, ensuring that your family has what they need to succeed. As you throw off passivity, you can take the initiative to see that your family is flourishing. In the process, the Lord is shaping your own leadership skills.

FOR REFLECTION AND APPLICATION

1. Can you identify with the husband who knows that he should lead but doesn't know where he is going? What are some goals you have for your family? What are some plans you are making to achieve those goals?
2. Is your home generally "well managed"? Are people working together, and are problems resolved? What are some talents within your family, and what are you doing to make sure they are being cultivated?
3. Why must leaders learn the art of delegation? How are you delegating responsibilities in your home or your church and then following up?
4. Does your wife feel like she is on your team? Have you actively sought to encourage her in her gifting? Do the members of your ministry team feel encouraged?
5. Do you tend to be impatient with others? How does it come out? Are you tempted to patiently go in circles without a clear goal? No matter your leadership position in the church, is your job description clear? Are your hoped-for outcomes clear in your mind?

6

LEARNING TO COMMUNICATE

The Lord God has given me the tongue of those who are instructed to know how to sustain the weary with a word. (Isa. 50:4 CSB)

Our church plant was struggling in its early days. I took these problems as a prompt to step away from the day-to-day and pray about our direction. Over time, the Lord began to give me ideas and plans that I knew would help us. I came back from that retreat encouraged and excited. When they heard my thoughts, the elders were on board. But when we presented the proposal to the congregation, there were questions and opposition.

"Why?" I asked my wife that night. "What went wrong?"

"You did not bring us along in your thinking," she insightfully observed. "You just announced the changes and expected us to go along. That's not how people work."

From that day forward, "bring us along in your thinking" became a byword in our house. I had learned a painful lesson: A leader must communicate. As Mohler writes, "To be human is to communicate, but to be a leader is to communicate constantly, skillfully, intentionally, and strategically."[1]

1. Albert Mohler, *The Conviction to Lead: 25 Principles for Leadership That Matters* (Bethany House, 2012), 91.

Leading God's family requires excellent and clear communication. Our biological household gives us a perfect place to learn these skills. In this chapter, we will focus on five different ways we can grow in the proficient use of words. We will look first at how a leader can communicate to the whole. Then we will think about how to interact personally. Next we will examine how to improve our teaching skills. In the last two sections, we will consider how shepherding our families and our wives gives us a chance to grow in vital pastoral skills.

LEARNING TO COMMUNICATE TO THE WHOLE

Therefore encourage one another and build one another up, just as you are doing. (1 Thess. 5:11)

Your words are powerful tools for teaching, encouraging, and challenging those you lead. The absence of skillful words hinders your leadership. My own story in the beginning of this chapter painfully illustrates that point. Early on in my ministry, I realized I desperately needed to grow in this vital area. I did not understand people or how to influence them. That's not a very good characteristic of a pastor! The following are some lessons I learned that can help you lead both your home and your church.

Communicate vision. A good leader uses words to cast a positive vision. For a family, this could be as simple as "We want to have a loving family" or "In our family, we want to display God's love to the world." Whether children or adults, all of us need to be reminded of why we are doing what we are doing. Restating the vision is motivating.

This applies to the church you are leading. Tell your people over and over how you believe God is using them or wants to use them. For example, right now our church is seeking to refurbish a building that "we can grow into and plant out of." We are regularly reminded of that vision. Someone has wisely observed, "When you are tired of saying the vision, people are just beginning to hear it."

Communicate strategy. It is one thing to communicate a vision for our families or churches. But how are we going to accomplish the vision? Communicating the plan tells us how. For example, you might say, "We have people over at our house for hospitality to show them the love of Christ. When you help Mom and me with the chores before they arrive, you are showing them the love of Christ. Could you help me set the table please?" Strategy puts the vision into action.

Communicate encouragement and affirmation. Life is discouraging. The word *encourage* connotes the idea of putting courage into someone for the future, while affirmation appreciates what they have done in the past. In our example above, we might say, "You have done such a good job helping me recently. You are growing up!"

A ministry leader must consistently encourage and affirm his people in a discouraging world. We set the temperature of the group we lead. All of us respond best to encouragement. Mark Dever observes, "So many times I've seen men, particularly younger guys, act as if real leadership is shown in correcting others. That's why young men's sermons often scold. What they haven't figured out is that you can often accomplish more by encouragement. There are times to scold. But 80 to 90 percent of what you hope to correct can be accomplished through encouragement."[2]

Are you a skilled encourager, giving grace with your words? Or are you stingy with your praise? Do you recognize the achievements of others? Both children and adults blossom under specific, consistent encouragement. Even a simple "Thank you for serving!" does wonders for a person's heart.

Communicate persuasively. You may not have thought of this as a skill to develop. But if we understand persuasion to be "the act of influencing the mind by arguments or reasons offered,"[3] then a pastor

2. Mark Dever, *Discipling: How to Help Others Follow Jesus* (Crossway, 2016), 101.
3. *Websters Dictionary 1828—Online Edition,* s.v. "persuasion," accessed April 14, 2025, https://webstersdictionary1828.com/Dictionary/persuasion.

is persuading in all of his ministry. You may be seeking to convince in a counseling situation, a sermon, a team meeting, or a congregational business meeting.[4] Persuasion assumes that you know what people find compelling, motivating, and reasonable. The opening story for this chapter revealed my blind spot of needing to persuade or "bring people along in my thinking."

We can learn this vital skill as we shepherd our older children. Although there are times when I appeal to my authority as a dad, I want to increasingly appeal to the thinking of my older children. God tells us, "Sweetness of speech increases persuasiveness" (Prov. 16:21); a perfect place to practice and grow in this skill is at home.

Communicate through trials and transition. As a leader in my family and church, I have a unique perspective. My words and emotional stability matter as I pilot our ship through storms. Whether it is a family adjusting to a health-related trial or a congregation adjusting to changes to numerical growth, there will be challenges and transitions. I can help those I lead see the positive side of the changes, and I can assure them of God's presence amid each trial. Your times of teaching and counsel help your family and church know how to interpret confusing circumstances.

Even as I write this chapter, I am watching a pastor lead his flock through the rebuilding process after a natural disaster destroyed their church building and homes. He is giving hope to his people through his presence and his direction. He is also reminding them about God's goodness and sovereignty. Jesus's care and presence are communicated to his people through the presence of an undershepherd. As one insightful pastor's wife remarked to her husband, "In a crisis, when you show up, people sense that God has shown up." A good pastor helps us know how to think in times of difficulty. We need to be reminded of God's care and promises when we are going through painful trials.

4. For examples of Paul persuading, see Acts 17:4; 18:4, 13; 19:8, 26.

Leading God's households well means becoming increasingly skilled at communicating with the whole. A godly father uses the power of his words to build up and guide his family. A godly pastor serves his people by doing the same.

LEARNING TO COMMUNICATE TO THE INDIVIDUAL

Do not let any unwholesome talk come out of your mouths, but only what is helpful for building others up according to their needs, that it may benefit those who listen. (Eph. 4:29 NIV)

While communicating vision and encouragement to the whole family is important, so is the ability to speak carefully and skillfully to individuals. Yet for something as powerful and ubiquitous as talking, we can be remarkably unskilled with our words. We talk too much or not enough. We speak in a way that is unclear, at a moment that is not effective, or in a tone that is not appropriate. We need help! Your wife and your children can help you grow in this area.

Over time, by trial and error, my emotional intelligence and communication skills have increased. By God's grace, I have learned good questions to ask. I have become more encouraging and more patient. I have learned to lead individuals through change with good communication. I understand more clearly how pleasant words can calm a conflict. Not only does this make me a wiser husband, but it also makes me a wiser shepherd. I know how to speak more effectively to men and women who are troubled or fearful.

Because you are a shepherd, what you say matters. Individuals will replay your words over and over. Every so often one of my adult children will tell me, "Dad, I can still hear your voice in my head." Our words are powerful! The more ably you communicate with others, the more trust you will gain and the more effective you will be. If God has called you to lead, then he has called you to communicate skillfully. And your wife and children are the perfect ones to help you grow in this area.

What are some communication lessons you can learn in the home?

First, start with listening. A wise shepherd draws out the purposes of another and listens before speaking (see Prov. 18:13; 20:5). He learns to ask questions, listen, and then ask more questions. Something as simple as this can go a long way: "So if I am hearing you correctly, you are saying ________. Am I understanding your concern?" As a husband and pastor, I had to learn to listen in such a way that the other person not only *is* heard but *feels* heard.

Second, use skillful words that fit the need of the moment. Our words can deliver grace and encouragement in the home and to individuals in the church. Sometimes a skillful correction may be needed. Even in tense moments, our word choice itself is important (see Prov. 12:18; 15:23). Words are the primary tools with which we may build up our wives, our children, and our church members. And being quick to ask forgiveness when you should is vitally important. We will deal more with the topic of forgiveness in the following chapter.

Third, consider not only what you say but how it might be received. Does it give grace to the hearers? Though it's not always possible to know, we must remember that there is often a difference between what we say and what others hear. I once said in a sermon, "Many times we are just dumb sheep." A young man approached me afterward visibly upset. After I inquired as to the reason, he explained, "When I was a child, my father often used to tell me I was dumb." From that incident I learned to think carefully about the words I chose. As far as it is up to us, we want to speak such that we cannot be misunderstood. It is not enough to think about the intent of our words. We also need to consider their impact.

Finally, understand that the medium is the message. Our countenance and our tone communicate so much to our wives and children. Delivering hard news with sadness in our voices and faces can take some of the sting away, just as our smiles can make their day. Similarly, in the church, face-to-face and voice communication trump texts and emails every time. How many hard conversations should have been had in-person rather than via text? Yet human nature prefers the path of least resistance and confrontation. As a pastor, if I received a critical email, I would immediately stop reading it and call the sender, asking him to tell me his concern over the phone. As I used to say to my team, "Good news in writing. Bad news in person."

God has given his image bearers the valuable ability to build others up through our words. Grow in that skill by practicing with your wife and children. You will lead God's households well as you grow increasingly skillful in your interpersonal communication.

LEARNING TO TEACH SKILLFULLY

And these words that I command you today shall be on your heart. You shall teach them diligently to your children, and shall talk of them when you sit in your house, and when you walk by the way, and when you lie down, and when you rise. (Deut. 6:6–7)

As leaders, we use our words not only to influence in general but also to instruct. If you are a pastor, then teaching the Word of God is the primary way you influence. Teaching is both a gift from God and a skill to develop. After leading one of my first Bible studies, an older woman gently said to me in private, "Hon, I had no idea what you were saying tonight." I was supposed to be teaching God's people the Word of God. And I needed to get better at it!

As pastors, we want to instruct such that our listener is not only informed but also transformed. To bring this about, a master teacher or preacher is always growing in his craft. He is simultaneously evaluating the material, the capability of his students, and the best way to promote understanding. And who can help us grow in this skill? Our children!

Teaching your children the gospel and the Scriptures is one of your main responsibilities as a dad. God commands you to teach and talk about him (see Deut. 6:7; Eph. 6:4). Thus a man who wants to be an example to his church and raise children who are faithful to the Lord will spend time evangelizing them and teaching them.

Fulfilling this duty may express itself in a number of different ways. It may involve leading family devotions or making sure that we have individual spiritual conversations with our children.[5] It may involve teaching them a catechism or apologetics materials. It will mean that we have delegated some of this instruction to others. But as the pastor of my house, I know the importance of instruction, and I should do everything in my power to promote biblical knowledge.

Even as we fulfill our fatherly duties to teach our children, God can simultaneously train us to be better teachers. Children give us immediate feedback if they find our teaching confusing or boring! Learning to simplify the material for their understanding helps me. In my preaching preparation, I would often ask myself, "How can I explain this passage to my children?" This helped me process the material I had studied so that I could be succinct, precise, concrete, and practical. Once your main message is clear enough to be understood by a child, then you can elaborate for adults. Martin Luther taught this way, saying, "Preach to the milkmaids and the doctors will be edified."

Teaching children can also train you to use effective illustrations. Jesus, the master teacher, employed stories, object lessons, natural phenomena, proverbs, and questions to help instruct his disciples. Too often our teaching can be like serving a prime piece of steak, raw and in big chunks. It's high quality but hard to digest. How much better to serve a finely prepared meal.

Improving our teaching could also be as simple as asking your wife or another leader, "What is one specific way you think I could improve as a preacher or teacher?" As pastors of God's households, we are leading well if we are instructing those under our care in the Word and doing so with increasing skill.

5. See Chap Bettis, *The Disciple-Making Parent: A Comprehensive Guidebook for Raising Your Children to Love and Follow Jesus Christ* (Diamond Hill Publishing, 2016), chapters 14, 15, and 16, where I elaborate more on this.

LEARNING TO SHEPHERD BETTER

As you know, like a father with his own children, we encouraged, comforted, and implored each one of you to walk worthy of God, who calls you into his own kingdom and glory. (1 Thess. 2:11–12 CSB)

Pastoring includes teaching, but it is more than teaching. A pastor is a physician of the souls under his care, studying them and seeking to present them mature in Christ (see Col. 1:28). We shepherd under the chief Shepherd (see 1 Peter 5:4)—caring for others like him, even as we ourselves are cared for by him. Christ patiently ministered to the bruised while also challenging the hard-hearted (see Luke 10:13–17; John 3:1–15). Paul commended that Christlike discernment when he encouraged the church to minister differently depending on the needs of each person. "And we urge you, brothers, admonish the idle, encourage the fainthearted, help the weak, be patient with them all" (1 Thess. 5:14).

A good pastor not only teaches but also encourages, counsels, and admonishes with the Word of God. His counsel is both public and private, planned and spontaneous. As he ministered to the Thessalonians, Paul sometimes encouraged them, sometimes comforted them, and other times implored them. A shepherd is one who applies the wisdom that a soul needs. This care does not come from a mere lecturer but from one who is knowledgeable and discerning about the beloved sheep under his care. Paul knew the Thessalonians individually. He had cared for *each one* of them.

Parenting gives us an opportunity to grow in all these qualities. Yes, as mentioned above, we instruct our children. We must also learn to ask them effective questions, both for our own understanding and for their understanding of themselves.[6] We are called to study them, delight in them, encourage them, and warn them. When my own son had a brain tumor, I knew that I needed to care for each of the

6. See Bettis, *Disciple-Making Parent*, chapters 10, 11, and 12, for more help with communication and questions.

members of my family. How were my wife and children processing this sudden trial? What Scriptures would we cling to? How was each one uniquely struggling amid this time of suffering? It was important to guide my family through this situation, not just as a group but also by talking with each individual to assess the unique needs of their hearts. And after several surgeries, we all weathered the storm—both physically and spiritually.

Studying my children helped shape my understanding of people in general. Seeing my children's struggles and motivations gave me insight into the inner workings of others. One child's deceptiveness gave concrete, albeit simple, insight into the deceptiveness of every human heart. Another's stubbornness reminded me of this same quality in many adults. And a third child's love of others' approval helped me practice ministering to that particular type of sin. Much of the human heart is the same, whether one is young or old. As my first secretary said to me, "In many ways adults are like children. They just hide it better."

Just as you are called to help individuals progress in the faith, so you are called to do all you can to present your children mature. This starts with clearly presenting the gospel to them and looking for the work of the Holy Spirit in their hearts. It also involves seeking to understand the situation they are in and the thoughts of their heart. Then it means applying one particular Scripture to one particular need. Good pastoring does the same.

You are managing your households well if you are growing increasingly skilled in pastoring all those in your care.

LEARNING TO SHEPHERD OUR SISTERS

The twelve were with him, and also some women . . . : Mary, called Magdalene, . . . and Joanna, the wife of Chuza, . . . and Susanna, and many others, who provided for them out of their means. (Luke 8:1–3)

In addition to caring for your children, you cannot lose sight of one valuable ally in learning to shepherd—your wife. Though the office of pastor/elder is limited to men, some leaders can treat the church as a fraternity. Women are treated as second-class citizens. They can be overlooked or taken for granted. However, a quick survey of the Gospels reveals that although only men were called as apostles, women were valued and honored by Jesus. They were his friends. And he trusted them to be the first witnesses of his resurrection. The early church, due to its care and protection of women, stood in sharp contrast with the Roman culture that did not value women. Our churches should strive to create the same environment.

The women in your church are a treasure and should feel treasured. As those made in God's image, purchased by Christ, and uniquely gifted by him, Jesus honored the women who followed him. He listened to them, taught them, and dined with them. They felt comfortable interacting with their Teacher. Some even traveled with him and supported him financially (see Luke 8:2–3). As we seek to reflect our chief Shepherd, we, too, want our teaching and conversation to communicate to the women under our care that they are valuable and that we understand them. Our wives can help us start learning this relational wisdom. Some of that insight will come as you seek to shepherd her. One pastor said to me, "Helping my wife follow Jesus teaches me how to help women in my church do the same." Another pastor commented, "My wife has helped me see things from a woman's perspective, which is helpful both in pastoring and preaching."

The results can be powerful. After one sermon, someone remarked to me, "I felt like you had read my journal." In other words, I not only explained the text but also explained her emotions. Good pastoring gives words to our sentiments. Learning to understand your wife can give you greater relational wisdom to interact with other women in your church. This wisdom will deepen both your counsel and your teaching.

But this insight will only come if you value your wife and honor her. Do you deem her worthy of your study? She has unique concerns, anxieties, and dreams. As you talk with, ask questions of, listen to, and study this daughter of Eve, you can shepherd her better. Your counsel and encouragement, which may now be simplistic, will grow in their effectiveness. You will learn particular Scriptures that help her. And that, in turn, will help you as you care for other women as well.

You are managing your households well if you are growing increasingly skilled in pastoring the women in your care.

CONCLUSION

The God of the universe cares for us through his living Word. He extends that care through the words of individuals like you and me. What an honor! Over time, I learned to "bring people along in my thinking," and so can you. Let's resolve to become increasingly skilled in using the tools God has given us to shepherd both our household and his.

FOR REFLECTION AND APPLICATION

1. How is your family-wide communication? Do you take opportunities to cast vision, direct, and encourage? Do you bring your family along in your thinking? Ask your wife for feedback.
2. Which of the communication lessons do you most need to learn? Would your wife and others agree? Plan a time to ask them.
3. As a man, do you feel responsible to instruct your children in the Word? What is your plan to do that? How has teaching your children made you a better teacher in the church?
4. How can pastoring your children well keep you from clumsily pastoring the flock? What are some lessons you are learning about people as you care for the individual needs of your children?
5. Would your wife say that you care for and shepherd her well? Is she flourishing under your care?

7

LEARNING TO LEAD IN CONFLICT

I do not ask for these only, but also for those who will believe in me through their word, that they may all be one, just as you, Father, are in me, and I in you, that they also may be in us, so that the world may believe that you have sent me. (John 17:20–21)

"Let's go visit Dan and Dana and see if they can help out with this."

Our first year of marriage was not shaping up the way I thought it would. The highs were dynamic, but the lows were devastating. When two strong-willed and passionate individuals try to establish a home after a quick engagement and inadequate premarital counseling, conflict is inevitable. Add an opinionated and impatient husband to the mix, and it's like pouring gasoline on the fire.

On this particular night, the conflict was over money. Finances were tight. Living with few pennies to spare was not easy. Any overspending, no matter how small, was a cause of tension. So Sharon and I found ourselves in the midst of another disagreement. We both agreed that we needed counsel, and so we headed out to visit some friends from our church. In fact, we headed out so quickly that we left the pumpkin bread baking. To make our embarrassment complete that night, we had to call our landlord and ask him to turn off the oven!

But God blessed our humility. By his grace, we prevented a fire in the kitchen and put out a fire in our marriage.

As I began writing this chapter on conflict and started considering all the situations I could describe, numerous stories flooded my mind. I could relay working through disagreements with my elder team. They were a godly group of men, but we saw things differently at times. Or what about the significant church disagreements we have confronted over the years? Then, of course, having parented teenagers, I could recount the storms Sharon and I survived in that realm. That would make for interesting reading! This is not even to mention the conflicts Sharon and I have had in our marriage.

When sinners live with other sinners, sparks will fly. And leading a group of sinners in God's family will mean that we need to both encourage unity and steward conflict. Our homelife can teach us those skills. In this chapter, we will think about encouraging love and unity, learning the art of healthy conflict, thinking about forgiveness, and developing a backbone. Let's look at these one at a time.

LEARNING TO ENCOURAGE LOVE AND UNITY

I appeal to you, brothers, by the name of our Lord Jesus Christ, that all of you agree, and that there be no divisions among you, but that you be united in the same mind and the same judgment. (1 Cor. 1:10)

Where two or three are gathered, there will be conflict. Church leaders spend an inordinate amount of time dealing with disagreements. Sometimes those disagreements may come from resistance to a change you are proposing. At other times, you will be coaching members on how to handle problems in their family, with their roommate, or at work. In addition, conflict might arise from your own lack of wisdom in handling a hurting or argumentative soul.

Good church leadership is constantly resolving conflict that should not be happening and initiating "conflict" that should. A survey of Paul's letters reveals both actions. At times he created tension by correcting sinful doctrine and living. At other times he was pleading for the church to overlook minor differences and remain unified. As a shepherd in both my family and my church, I too will be doing both. When the matter is of vital importance, I will need the backbone to lead well into the tension. But in other situations, I will be urging forbearance and forgiveness.

It is not just the minimization of conflict that we want. Unity is much more than that. Unity is oneness. It is being joined in mind and purpose with a supernatural love for each other. Our God is a tri-unity—diverse in his persons yet united in his essence. A unified and loving church or team is also diverse and united, and, as a result, it brings glory to God. Jesus taught that our love and unity testify of him (see John 13:34–35; 17:20–21).

Our home gives us a perfect chance to cultivate this unity. It can seem like a place of constant conflict. How is it that a younger sibling can expertly pester her older brother until he retaliates and gets into trouble? Why is it that the toy that was neglected for weeks suddenly has two children fighting over it today? Why is it that the teenager who had little interest in fashion now wants to wear something that I think is too revealing? Overseeing your home well will mean resolving lots of conflict—and reconciling lots of siblings.

How do you encourage unity in the home?

Value and communicate a vision for it. Jesus let his disciples overhear him praying for unity (see John 17:20–21). A survey of Paul's letters shows how often he urged the churches to aim for it.[1] He valued unity and regularly communicated its importance to the churches he planted. Like-mindedness in the home is equally important. Proverbs 17:1 tells us that it is better to be poor while enjoying domestic peace than to be rich while living with family strife. As just one way of casting this vision, I would often encourage my children, "Hey guys, the Lord says that it

1. For just a few verses on division, see Rom. 16:17; 1 Cor. 3:1–4; 6:1–11; 11:18–19; Gal. 5:19–20; and James 3:13–4:3. For a few verses on unity, see John 13:34–35; 17:23; 1 Cor. 1:10; and Eph. 4:3.

is good and pleasant when brothers and sisters live together in unity. That's our goal!" As a dad, I was regularly reminding my children that I wanted our home to be loving and unified. I was casting a vision for us to have an all-for-one and one-for-all attitude. We should speak of how much we value true unity in our homes.

As church leaders, we will need to value and communicate the same vision. Like Paul, we must urge others to maintain the unity of the Spirit (see Eph. 4:3). We ought to value and treasure harmony in our church. This unity is not a shallow uniformity; it does not mean that we never passionately disagree. But it does mean that in any disagreement that occurs, we remind one another how much Jesus values the unity of his followers.

Practice and teach the principles of conflict resolution. A vision for living together must translate into practical steps both before and during conflict. Healthy unity does not come from ignoring disagreements but from working through them in a God-glorifying manner. And where can we learn to practice the basics of biblical conflict resolution? In the home. At home and in the church, conflict is inevitable. Destructive conflict is not. The Bible is filled with instructions on dealing with discord. Most people are unaware of these principles and need to be taught them.[2]

Resolving conflict might include asking some of the following questions: Can I overlook this? Have I looked for the log in my own eye? Have I talked with the other person in private? What gracious words are called for in this situation? In what ways have I contributed to the problem? Do I, as the leader, need to apologize and ask forgiveness for something? Does someone else need to do so? Is this problem big enough that I need to involve a third party? These are just a few of the biblical principles we can teach others.

2. Ken Sande's *The Peacemaker: A Biblical Guide to Resolving Personal Conflict*, 3rd ed. (Baker, 2004) is the classic work and should be studied by every pastor; Ken Sande and Kevin Johnson's *Resolving Everyday Conflict* (Baker, 2015) is the shorter version.

As the leader of a home or a church, you must regularly teach these conflict resolution skills to others and apply them to the situations you face. To do this, you must clearly understand biblical principles for stewarding disagreements.

I use all these skills as I lead my family. Correctly handling a conflict between two preteen siblings might involve questions to investigate the facts, a judgment of who was at fault, and a plan for reconciliation. If I am the one who sinned against my children, then I will be the one asking for forgiveness, even as I continue to lead the family.

You are managing your households well when you encourage a genuine unity.

LEARNING THE ART OF HEALTHY CONFLICT

And the Lord's servant must not be quarrelsome but kind to everyone, able to teach, patiently enduring evil, correcting his opponents with gentleness. God may perhaps grant them repentance leading to a knowledge of the truth, and they may come to their senses and escape from the snare of the devil, after being captured by him to do his will. (2 Tim. 2:24–26)

It is much easier to coach others in stewarding conflict than it is to handle personal disagreements that are aimed at me. When I am the one accused of wrongdoing, it is easy for fear, defensiveness, or argumentativeness to take over. Early on in ministry, I had to learn not to be unnerved by conflict. I often just wanted it to "go away" so that we could get on with "the Lord's agenda." It took me years to realize that sometimes stewarding a disagreement well *is* the Lord's agenda—indeed, it's an oft-neglected way through which we may glorify God in the church.

Handling conflict in a healthy way calls for biblical and relational wisdom. Why? Because there are so many ways to *mishandle* disagreements. You can use words clumsily. You can be too aggressive and domineering or too passive and fearful. You can address unimportant matters too quickly when they should have just been ignored. Or you can delay when you need to speak. Sometimes overlooking an offense is a sign of godliness and love (see 1 Peter 4:8). Sometimes it is a sign of cowardice and passivity (see Gal. 2:12). At times, speaking sharply is a form of godly rebuke (see Rev. 3:19). At other times, it is a foolish and fleshly reaction (see Prov. 12:18). Should we forbear with a weakness, or should we exhort? Handling disagreements in a healthy way requires a backbone of steel, the wisdom of Solomon, and the heart of a child.

These were some of the hardest lessons to learn. In the second year of our church plant, I could sense some storm clouds brewing with an older man in the congregation. But I procrastinated taking him out for coffee to talk because I hated the idea of conflict. The blowup would have been much smaller if I had taken the loving initiative sooner. At other times, I have listened to the words a person was speaking but failed to hear the hurt behind them. Addressing the hurt so that they felt known and loved would have dissolved much of the disagreement. At still other times, I was in a battle for control of the church when there was gossip and manipulation, and it required that I have the courage to confront.

While the previous section encouraged you to cast a corporate vision for unity and biblical conflict resolution, we also need to think about how we handle disagreements that are close to home. Marriage gives us a perfect chance to learn those skills! Over my years of ministry, Sharon has helped me become a better pastor. Some of that improvement has come through her insights about me amid some of our own conflicts. Other benefits have come as I have learned to care for and confront her in the inevitable ups and downs of married life. In the process of caring for your wife properly, you can grow to become a better shepherd of God's household.

Whether in marriage or in ministry, God calls us to move toward the conflict—even when it is aimed at us. Mature leaders take the initiative to be peacemakers (see Matt. 5:9). At times, we may overlook sinful words that don't characterize a person (see Eccl. 7:21–22). At other times, we may seek to grow personally, asking, "What do you think I am not seeing?" Or we may realize that we have done all we can and leave it in the Lord's hands (see Rom. 12:18). But navigating personal conflict requires humble discernment and a lot of prayer. I can think of several young pastors who might still be in ministry if they had humbly listened to the critiques that some fellow leaders had given them. Instead, they were defensive and inflexible, inflaming the disagreement.

Conflict is inevitable in both the home and the church. But rather than allowing it to tear you down, working through it can lead to even greater unity. Loving your wife amid the inevitable friction of married life is a great place to learn this art of stewarding disagreements. You will need it in the church.

You are managing your households well when you can disagree in a healthy way.

LEARNING TO FORGIVE AND FORBEAR

Be kind to one another, tenderhearted, forgiving one another, as God in Christ forgave you. (Eph. 4:32)

"Why didn't they offer a class, or even a lecture, on forgiveness at seminary?" I wondered. I was trying to recover from a deeply critical conversation with a longtime member. I had expended great personal effort to bless her family. But in the end, she disparaged both my effort for her *and* my preaching. I felt like an NFL quarterback who had been blindsided by a three-hundred-pound defensive tackle.

"Ugh!" I thought. "Can I go on?"

I think every pastor knows those situations. You lay yourself out for the cause of Christ. You're not asking to be thanked. Giving to others is part of the job. But in those exhausted moments, you don't want to be kicked when you are down. And then it happens. Sometimes the painful incident occurs when you have the least capacity to bear it. Whether you are leading in the home or in the church, there will be many moments when you will need to practice forgiveness and forbearance. And you will need to teach others to do the same.

Forbearance is not a word we often use today, but it is a biblical fruit of the Spirit. Forbearance means overlooking a sin or an annoyance. We see this in our Savior as he bore with the lack of understanding and pettiness of the disciples. He taught us that even now, God is kind to the evil and ungrateful every time he causes it to rain (see Matt. 5:45; Luke 6:35). He continues to forbear with *our* ongoing sin and missteps. We must emulate his forbearance as we live in a sin-soaked world. As parents, a key component of our work is encouraging our children to think the best of others and overlook small offenses. That includes forbearing with *us*! Since God has overlooked our sins on the cross, our love for others covers a multitude of sins (see 1 Peter 4:8). We must teach our church family and our biological family that it is our glory to overlook an offense (see Prov. 19:11).

Some sins, however, are so great that they cannot and should not be merely overlooked. Those we must forgive as a deliberate act of the will. Learning to forgive is an essential skill of family life and church life. In the Lord's Prayer, Jesus presented forgiveness as a daily need—we daily need to forgive and be forgiven. We can absorb the pain of an offense and mark it canceled by the power of the Spirit. We do this not because of the worthiness of the recipient but because of the forgiveness we ourselves have received (see Matt 18:21–35). Understanding both the Bible's standards for our behavior and the magnitude of our own indwelling sin, Christians should also be able to ask forgiveness of each other easily. Nowhere is this need more prevalent than in the home. A godly home is not one of shiny perfection but one where individuals ask and extend forgiveness.

The idea of forbearance can be helpful to both the parent and the pastor or elder. We will often see plenty of ways our children can grow. But where do we start? Discernment informs our care for them so that even though there is much to work on, we focus only on one or two issues at a time. We forbear with the rest. Pastoral counseling also requires that same discernment and prioritization.

As a shepherd of both households, I am going to be regularly reminding and teaching individuals to forgive and forbear. Most importantly, if I am going to stay in ministry long-term, I must practice those same graces.

You are managing your households well when you master forgiveness as an important outworking of compassion and grace.

LEARNING TO HAVE BACKBONE

Have I not commanded you? Be strong and courageous. (Josh. 1:9)

With sweating hands and a racing heart, I picked up the phone. An older woman had become dissatisfied with our church and left for another church. I accepted it, thinking, "That's all just part of living in a fallen world." Except she kept attending one of our women's Bible studies even as she continued to criticize the current church leadership. I had known her for years, but I needed to intervene. I was dreading the call because I had encountered her sharp tongue before. With a prayer for courage, I dialed the number and started the conversation.

The willingness to confront is a necessary competency for leadership. A hard conversation must be had with skill, patience, gentleness, thoughtfulness, and prayerfulness. But it must be had. Our Savior was willing to speak truthfully even when it did not please his listeners. He moved calmly among hostile crowds and authorities. His Spirit can help us develop this same courage. How? We often grow in fortitude as we move toward hard discussions. Over time, I have learned to initiate difficult conversations rather than procrastinating. There were many conversations like the one described above, whether over the phone or in person, when my mouth was dry and I was nervous. I took comfort in the quip by the late John Wayne, "Courage is being scared to death and saddling up anyway."

Leaders need backbone. Good leadership, at times, means making decisions that some don't agree with. Though we want to be humble, winsome, communicative leaders, we do not want to be like Aaron, living in fear of the people and simply doing their bidding. We want to be convictional without being pugilistic, and humble without being spineless, acting with manly firmness.

One place we can learn to stand firm is in our homes. Our wives, our greatest counselors, are also flawed. They are not always right any more than we are. This is where loving leadership can falter. When our homelife is tense, it is tempting to sinfully acquiesce. As the popular saying goes, "If Mama ain't happy, ain't nobody happy."

However, Scripture is clear: Adam should not have listened to Eve at the moment of temptation (see Gen. 3:17); Abram should not have acquiesced to Sarai (see Gen. 16:2); Aaron should not have capitulated to the people (see Ex. 32:21); and Peter should not have given way to the Judaizers (see Gal. 2:12). Your servant leadership will not always make your wife or your children happy. Often we don't want to disappoint either of them, but we must beware lest servant leadership become servile leadership. Godly service involves leading them to the Lord and to love others. It sometimes means gently pressing against our wife's fears or sinful desires. It means leading the family where *God* wants it to go, even if it's not where your wife wants it to go at the moment.

We need this same firm leadership in the church. Although godly leadership will generally lead to respect, there will be occasions when we must make unpopular decisions that will not please the crowd. There were times when people were less than happy with my decisions. I had to learn how to be humble and teachable—*and* stay true to my convictions. Our leadership team had to learn how to love those with embittered pasts or strong personalities without letting them take over the church. In one particular instance, we made a decision to stop having our beloved church retreat. The retreat center could not handle our growing church, prices had increased, and what once had been a meaningful spiritual experience had become mostly a social time. There was quite a bit of grumbling at the decision, even though certain individuals later admitted that they knew it was the right one.

A godly husband and shepherd will lead with humble conviction, carefully listening to others. He will seek to communicate gently, kindly, and winsomely. But ultimately, he will seek to please the Lord, not men and women. That will mean enduring some times at home or at church when there is a "chill in the room."

You are managing your households well when you embrace hard assignments and hard conversations as a leader.

CONCLUSION

Leading a united church is a joy. Yet, that unity will only come as the Spirit empowers us to handle our inevitable disagreements in a God-glorifying way. God's Word provides numerous principles that equip us to walk through conflict in a way that honors him. The gospel also provides the motivation and the power to forgive and be reconciled. A godly leader has learned to equip his people in these areas. How blessed are those under his care.

FOR REFLECTION AND APPLICATION

1. Is your family united? Have you accepted ongoing sinful disagreements as normal? How would studying biblical principles of conflict resolution help you glorify the Lord amid conflict?
2. Have you thought of stewarding conflict as a skill you need to learn? What biblical and practical lessons have you learned over the years? What skills can you learn or grow in at home?
3. Do you understand the biblical motives for and methods of forgiveness? What resources could help you grow in this understanding?
4. How good are you at handling hard conversations? Do you passively procrastinate or aggressively attack? How might you begin to grow in this area?

5. If you are a church leader, consider a time you had to stand up for what was right and make a church member (or two) unhappy as a result. What lessons did you learn from that time? What small acts of courage or conviction is God calling you to now?

8

LEARNING CHARACTER LESSONS

And we all, with unveiled face, beholding the glory of the Lord, are being transformed into the same image from one degree of glory to another. For this comes from the Lord who is the Spirit. (2 Cor. 3:18)

I walked out of our early morning elders' prayer time stunned. It had been my idea to take time to encourage and challenge each other personally. Specifically, I suggested that we speak to each other's strengths and weaknesses. We would encourage each other with positives, and we would challenge each other to grow in other areas. Some of those weaknesses we might have already known about, but perhaps we didn't realize the effect they were having on others. Other weaknesses might have been blind spots—areas we had no idea were impacting others. This exercise, we agreed, would help us all grow and serve better as elders.

As the lead pastor, I would go first. During that initial meeting, I listened carefully. I heard specific encouragement about my strengths. Then came detailed observations concerning my weaknesses. I knew about some of those issues, but others were new to me. We closed in prayer and then left for the morning. I felt a little tender, like I had just been through an invasive medical procedure.

The next week, we met again for prayer and discussion. But as the meeting progressed, the discussion that had taken a full hour for me only lasted fifteen minutes for each of the other elders. I was stunned! Why was I the focus of so much attention the previous week? Was I that much worse of a sinner than the rest?

In the days that followed, I prayed over those conversations. I knew these guys loved me, but I felt ganged up on. Slowly I realized that the heightened scrutiny came on account of my greater influence as the lead pastor. My strengths and weaknesses were more obvious. The question now was: How would I react to their pointed critiques? Would I listen and make changes, or would I be defensive? Eventually I came to the point where I was thankful for the critique. I wanted to grow. "Lord," I prayed, "I want to be the best I can be. Thank you for this input."

Leading God's households will challenge your character as well. You, too, can be stimulated to greater growth if you will be humble, teachable, and hungry to progress.

If you are not teachable, then the suggestions from the previous chapters of this book will have no value to you. Why point out the ways God intends to develop your relational wisdom if you don't think you need to grow?

But if you do have the heart to mature and fight complacency, then put the suggestions from the previous chapters into practice. And remember, while you can grow in skill as a leader, it is character that God cares about most. In this chapter, we will think about two vital ways of growing in your character as you lead both households.

LEAD WITH A CONTINUAL DESIRE TO GROW

Practice these things, immerse yourself in them, so that all may see your progress. (1 Tim. 4:15)

In an earlier chapter, I proposed that poor leadership is often better described as passable leadership. Neither poor nor excellent. Why is that? One of the biggest reasons, I believe, is that leaders reach a point of passable competency and then stop learning. With so many other demands, why seek to grow as a leader when things seem to be running "fine"?

The phrase "plateaued leader" was anathema to me when I was younger, and it still is today. I hope it is for you too. God wants us to continue growing throughout our ministry. Complacency is a temptation for all leaders, whether they are young, middle-aged, or older. It is far too easy to coast.

Would you like to fly in a commercial aircraft where the pilot's competency is merely adequate? Don't you want him to continue honing his skills and training for the inevitable storms that will come his way? Like this pilot, your actions and inactions affect others. The more people you lead, the more your weaknesses will be visible and will impact others. At times, the consequences will be caused by what you do and how you do it. At other times, they will result from what you don't do. But as a leader, you *will* impact others.

This is why we want to work on our weaknesses. Some of those flaws we know about; others we can't see. And why can't we see them? Because our self-awareness is affected by sin. Paul Tripp has written, "My self-perception is as accurate as a carnival mirror."[1] By very definition, we cannot see our own blind spots.

Do you have shortcomings that are negatively impacting others? Then why don't they tell you? They have probably tried! C. S. Lewis called these blind spots our fatal flaws:

> That is the next great step in wisdom—to realize that you also are just that sort of person. You also have a fatal flaw in your character. . . .
>
> It is no good passing this over with some vague, general admission such as "Of course, I know I have my faults." It is important to realize that there is some really fatal flaw in you:

1. Paul David Tripp, *Instruments in the Redeemer's Hands: People in Need of Change Helping People in Need of Change* (P&R Publishing, 2002), 54.

> something which gives the others just that same feeling of despair which their flaws give you. And it is almost certainly something you don't know about. . . . But why, you ask, don't the others tell me? Believe me, they have tried to tell you over and over again, and you just couldn't "take it."[2]

How do we avoid missing these fatal flaws? We listen to others!

A growing leader must be able to receive both critique and criticism without getting defensive. I define critique as a negative observation that comes from a "friendly" source, while criticism is one that comes from a "less than friendly" source. We should not be surprised by either. As Charles Spurgeon has said, "Public men must expect public criticism." The greater our influence, the more others will be able to identify our weaknesses.

Why is it that some leaders in the church can't receive critique or criticism without becoming defensive? No doubt there is pride, fear of man, and love of approval in the mix. But another reason may be that we don't think we can lead imperfectly and keep growing. Somewhere along the way, we may have believed the lie that we must lead without making mistakes. If someone suggests that we are falling short, we believe this person is attacking us personally; they are suggesting that *we* are inadequate.

I once knew a man in leadership who could not see his own flaws. He never admitted to doing the wrong thing or speaking the wrong word. I often wondered why. Was he like Ron in our introduction? Did he never think he was wrong? Or was he insecure in his leadership, believing that an apology would give others the upper hand? Working with him was like playing pickup basketball with a guy who never lets you call a foul. Eventually, his colleagues grew tired of interacting with him. And rather than sharpen each other like they were supposed to (see Prov. 27:17), it was easy for others

2. C. S. Lewis, *God in the Dock: Essays on Theology and Ethics*, ed. Walter Hooper (HarperCollins, 2014), chap. 18, ebook.

to withdraw and leave him alone. Like Ron in our introduction, they gave up trying to challenge him.

This is where your wife can help. In a healthy marriage, a wife both sees your weaknesses and loves you anyway. She can challenge you to keep growing as a leader. Certainly, we don't want soul-crushing criticism. Some wives can overcorrect and offer little—or no—encouragement. But no matter how it is delivered, we must be willing to hear correction. If you will humble yourself and lower your defenses, you will grow and mature as a leader.

In my own informal survey of current pastors, I received observations like these: "I have a lot of blind spots, but because of my wife, I have fewer, and the stubborn ones are less glaring to people." "She has made me less self-centered and more others-focused." "My wife has helped me become more compassionate, caring, thoughtful, and insightful with women." All these men have learned to invite and listen to the voices of their wives.

If your wife is one who avoids conflict and *only* encourages you, realize that this may not be healthy. A leader with this sort of wife may actually be in danger of not growing. Our wives are to be both encouragement-givers and hard-truth-speakers.[3] Ask your wife for her input. "What blind spots do I have that hinder my work as a pastor?"

In addition to your wife, invite input from others to help improve your leadership and shepherding. Let Spurgeon advise us again: "A sensible friend who will unsparingly criticize you from week to week will be a far greater blessing to you than a thousand indiscriminating admirers, if you have sense enough to bear his treatment and grace enough to be thankful for it."[4]

Other people see ways you could improve. They are just afraid to tell you. Ask them face-to-face, "How do you think I could improve

3. See Timothy Keller with Kathy Keller, *The Meaning of Marriage: Facing the Complexities of Commitment with the Wisdom of God* (Penguin, 2013). In chapter 5, "Loving the Stranger," Keller presents an excellent treatment of how our wives can both see our flaws and encourage us.

4. C. H. Spurgeon, *Lectures to My Students* (Hendrickson Publishers, 2010), 66.

as a leader?" By inviting their input, you are humbling yourself and admitting that you still need to grow—and that you desire to do so. You are being aggressively teachable, and like Timothy, your progress will be evident to all (see 1 Tim. 4:15).

God has given you people to strengthen you and challenge you. Invite the input of your wife and others to become the best shepherd you can be. You are managing your households well if you are humble, eager to grow, and willing to listen to critique and criticism.

LEARNING TO DIE TO YOURSELF

> *But whoever would be great among you must be your servant, and whoever would be first among you must be your slave, even as the Son of Man came not to be served but to serve, and to give his life as a ransom for many. (Matt. 20:26–28)*

If you want God to use you in his kingdom, you must learn to die to yourself. It is really that simple. Only when a kernel of wheat falls into the ground and dies does it produce fruit (see John 12:24). When you learn to embrace the ego-crushing tutelage of Jesus, then he can take you to higher planes of fruitfulness (see 2 Cor. 1:9).

Loving and leading any group of people, whether a church or a family, is ultimately done for an audience of One. Because Jesus loves you, you take care of his sheep in the home and in the church. Like Peter, your love for him leads you to love the people he loves. This attitude precludes any harsh or abusive leadership of your children or your wife. Even as you are called to love and lead your home, you are to do so as its chief servant.

Kingdom love inevitably involves death to self. My family is one vital place where I learn this. When I come home, do I pick up the servant's towel or the ruler's robe? Do I come home to serve or be served? There is nothing like marriage and parenting to reveal my own selfishness and desire to be served. As I interact with my wife and children, I can see my own impatience, laziness, and self-absorption. But it is also here that I can grow. As I learn to lead amid the messiness of family life, I am also developing the spiritual muscles for the often thankless sacrifice of pastoring.

As a young dad, I remember a conference speaker challenging me to think of coming home as arriving at my second-shift job. After this exhortation, I would sit in my driveway at the end of the day, thank the Lord for his grace up to that point, and then ask him to give me strength to serve my family well. With four children close in age and a small house, I often came into a glorious chaos. Sometimes there was conflict to referee, homework to help with, or clutter to corral. I didn't always handle the chaos in a godly way. Looking back, I cannot think of a time when Sharon and I were more exhausted—or happier!

Similarly, ministry to God's people is often inconvenient. It means continuing to serve even when we are bone-tired. It comes with criticisms and expectations that other callings don't have. We shoulder the cares and sorrows of many on our hearts (see 2 Cor. 11:28). We feel relational tension that others don't know about. We must act responsibly when others act childishly. We must extend forgiveness when others attack. We must pour love into relationships, even when others are making withdrawals. We must pursue individuals who will not appreciate it. True Christlike leadership means humbling ourselves and becoming a servant.

Yet in this servant leadership and death to self, there is also a tension. A wise overseer both denies himself and understands his ministry responsibilities. The same men who were taught to wash feet also recruited others to feed the widows (see Acts 6:1–4). Sometimes our self-denying service involves picking up the towel. Sometimes it involves delegating and coordinating. Servant leadership is always asking: "What is the best way for others to be served?"

Unfortunately, I have seen young leaders who think that Christian service should only take place during business hours. They seem to have a sense of entitlement, seeking to spend most of their time attending conferences, discussing theology over good coffee, and preparing sermons. Pastoring can seem like a sweet gig. Other leaders, whether from cynicism or weariness, minimize difficult conversations. Functionally they are withdrawn from the congregation, sending directives through others.

Brother, leading God's households involves hard *work*! Our Savior labored so hard in teaching and healing the crowds that he slept through a storm (see Matt. 8:24). Over and over again, Paul reminded his churches of his labor for them while calling their leadership to do the same.[5]

There is no place for laziness or lording in ministry. Like Christ Jesus, who took the nature of a servant and humbly served us, even to the point of death on a cross (see Phil. 2:6–8), we must humbly die to ourselves and serve others for the sake of his name. As servant-leaders in our homes and churches, we exemplify two of his qualities—*leadership* and self-denying *service*. You are managing your households well when you are both dying to yourself and leading well.

CONCLUSION

The main qualification God tells us to look for in potential leaders is character. Though none of us is perfect, do you have a heart that is teachable and that wants to grow? Are you willing to die to yourself, or do you want others to serve you? Until the Lord returns, we are to grow in grace and knowledge—and that includes leadership knowledge. Our families give us a daily opportunity to lead, learn, and love.

FOR REFLECTION AND APPLICATION

1. Do you realize you have blind spots that others see? Have you thought about how those blind spots affect others? How can you seek input from your wife and others?
2. How do you react to critique and criticism? Why is that?

5. For Scriptures on Paul's hard work, see Acts 20:35; 1 Cor. 15:10; 2 Cor. 6:4–5; 11:23; 1 Thess. 2:9; 2 Thess. 3:8.

3. Have you thought about how God is calling you to die to yourself even as you lead his people? In which areas of your life do you find this pattern difficult to implement?
4. Do you agree with the servant-leader tension the author presents? Would your wife and children say that you are a servant-leader? Do you tend to serve without initiating? Or do you tend to lead without picking up the towel?
5. Are you tempted toward entitlement or withdrawal? Why is that? Given the high calling of pastors, how can you progress in these areas?

CONCLUSION

By this all people will know that you are my disciples, if you have love for one another. (John 13:35)

We have come to the end of our time together. We started this journey by learning how God calls all men, but especially church officers, to manage their homes well. Following Christ should affect how we lead and love our nearest neighbors—namely, those in our families. Learning leadership lessons in our smaller household helps us develop the relational wisdom we need to lead God's larger household, the church. God emphasized one particular aspect of leading our home well: teaching our children to obey us while remaining connected to their hearts. In our current world of permissive parenting, this biblical emphasis is absolutely essential. Fostering obedience and connection in our homes develops the relational wisdom that will help us lead God's household well.

Finally, we spent considerable time in the second half of the book looking at particular competencies we can learn as we shepherd our children and our wives. If we have a hunger to grow, God can take us to higher levels of leadership skill, communication, and conflict resolution. But all of this depends on our desire to keep growing.

However, in our discussion about the *how* of managing well, we have not probed the deeper question of *why*. Why does God desire us to lead our families and churches well? Understanding the *why* can help keep us on track with the *how* over a lifetime.

So, just what are those deeper purposes? Let me suggest three: to glorify God, to serve others, and to train for eternity.

LEADING WELL GLORIFIES GOD

Scripture teaches that God created us for his glory (see Isa. 43:7). As the Westminster Shorter Catechism states in answer 1, "The chief end of man is to glorify God and enjoy him forever." Whether we eat or drink, we are to do all for the glory of God (see 1 Cor. 10:31).

However, for all the times we use the word *glory,* I think we are often unclear about what it means. This may be because Scripture uses this word in several different ways. For example, Scripture tells us that God *is* glorious. He is great, excellent, beautiful, awe-inspiring, and magnificent in his being.

In addition, the word *glory* can describe the visibility of God's magnificence and greatness. Though we can see some of God's glory in creation (see Ps. 19:1–2), we begin to see it most clearly in the person of Jesus. Further, at the Last Supper, Jesus specifically taught us that it was through the cross and the resurrection that God was glorified (see John 13:31–32). In the horrific event of the crucifixion, we start to comprehend a triune God who is holy, just, loving, humble, wise, and self-sacrificial.

On that same night, Jesus described another way God's glory could be seen. When his followers love each other as he loved them, the world begins to see Jesus (see John 13:34–35). They had watched him touch the leper, forgive the adulteress, eat with the outcast, and weep over the death of a friend. And how had he loved his disciples? He forgave their petty competition and overlooked their slow-wittedness. He recruited rough fishermen, a turncoat tax collector, and a nationalistic Zealot, and he expected them to call each other brothers. As his disciples, he calls us to do the same. A diverse group of people living together as a church family, loving Jesus, and loving each other is a sociological miracle. When this community is well-ordered, joyful, and truth focused, it displays the wisdom of God to the world and to the heavenly realm (see Eph. 3:10). It points to God's nature and to the coming consummation of the kingdom.

What is true of God's household is also true of our individual households. As we apply the gospel in our homes, we also point to our triune God and his coming kingdom. When we joyfully teach, love, discipline, encourage, and forgive, we are making the invisible God visible. This is true even when sinful storms come upon our families. In a sin-soaked world, a husband may break his marriage vows when trials hit. A wife may abandon her faith. A prodigal may reject his parents. Even then we can glorify God by handling those storms with trust, love, forgiveness, and kindness. We display the glory of God, not by living free from problems, but by handling them with his grace. Through the pain, we show the world that our highest hope is not in our earthly family but in our God.

LEADING WELL SERVES OTHERS

A loving, godly family has both a vertical purpose and a horizontal one. If you are in the child-rearing years, your days are likely filled with making sure homework is done and chauffeuring the kids to this week's sporting events. Based on the commitments you make for your children, the family schedule can become one good activity after another.

While raising children does demand a great deal of time, it does not demand *all* our time. We are teaching and discipling our children by what we prioritize. Augustine said that sin causes us to curve in on ourselves. This implies that even Christian families face the temptation to be self-focused. Parents can be child-centered. Unfortunately, the parents' marriage, church attendance, and dinner around the table all can take second place to the children's activities. Amid all this hustle, it can be easy to lose sight of another priority: serving others.

One reason we want to have a well-ordered family is so that we will be able to minister to others outside the family. Love *can* manage multiple priorities. A godly family will oppose self-focus and will have a love that spills out onto those in their church and community. Yet when a family has children or a schedule that is out of control, there is no energy to serve others. There is barely stamina to make it through the day.

A family without outward service is like a restaurant that never serves a customer. The employees may be well-managed and happy. The building could be clean and orderly. But no one outside the store is helped. Whether franchise or family, the whole purpose of being well-managed is to serve others.

Jesus taught his disciples, "It is more blessed to give than to receive" (Acts 20:35). He certainly modeled this as well. He is our perfect example of one who lived an earthly life in unhurried service to his Father and to those around him. This same principle of Christ-empowered service certainly applies to our families and our children. The crowning blessing on a well-led family is the ability to minister to others, whether they are inside or outside the church. Brother pastor, do you lead your family to minister to others? Or is ministry just a calling for you?

LEADING WELL TRAINS YOU FOR ETERNITY

Finally, we cannot overlook how God is developing *you*. When God created people in his image, he created them to rule and reign. Adam and Eve were given dominion, or rule, over the earth. They were told to fill it and to subdue it (see Gen. 1:28). Even before the fall, men and women were to cultivate and oversee the areas underneath their responsibility.

The entrance of sin into our world has not changed that original call; it has just made the call harder. Our relationships and our tasks are now filled with problems (see Gen. 3:16–19). Yet the call to oversee the areas of dominion, the fields God has given to us, still remains. One of the primary fields God gives us is our family. A home that is carefully and intentionally nurtured displays the wisdom of the parents. We cultivate and defend our families so that life can flourish.

In training us to lead and oversee well, God is also fitting us to rule and reign for eternity. Have you realized that you will be ruling in the new heavens and the new earth? The resurrected Jesus, the second Adam, has been installed in heaven and is reigning as king at this very minute. And who is his bride? The answer, of course, is the church! We are made to co-rule with him now and for all eternity. Paul tells us that "if we endure, we will also reign with him" (2 Tim. 2:12). And the book of Revelation declares that the saints will "reign forever and ever" (Rev. 22:5).

Our eternal existence will involve a lot more than just floating in the clouds! Randy Alcorn, writing about our call to rule and reign in heaven, states, "God is grooming us for leadership. He's watching to see how we demonstrate our faithfulness. He does that through his apprenticeship program, one that prepares us for Heaven. Christ is not simply preparing a place for us; he is preparing us for that place."[1] In the new heavens and the new earth, we will continue to manage and oversee.

Understanding this eternal trajectory helps us understand what God is doing in us right now. He is giving us small assignments on earth to train us for that eternal work (see Luke 19:11–27). Overseeing your household is a training ground for eternal oversight. Have you even considered that as you create a family and a home, God is giving you a little realm to rule underneath him? Part of growing in holiness includes learning to manage the fields God has given to us (see 2 Cor. 10:13–16). Are you stewarding that privilege well?

JAKE, RON, AND WILL

Let's return to Jake, Ron, and Will from our introduction. How would life have been different for them and their churches if the principles in this book had been implemented in their lives?

1. Randy Alcorn, *Heaven* (Tyndale, 2004), 215.

Jake would have taken his household leadership seriously and would have begun to apply these principles to church leadership. Even in seminary, with his mind immersed in theology and Greek, he also would have been reflecting on his need to grow as a shepherd of his home. Ron would have realized that just because he could domineer as a boss, that wasn't a godly way to relate to his wife or the flock. And Will, the loveable but passive husband, would have grown in initiating and proactively caring for those in his charge. His wife and children would be flourishing under his watchful care. All three of these men would have been intentional about how their leadership in their home glorified God, served others, and trained them to grow in holiness. Their painful church situations might have been avoided.

CONCLUSION

God has given you a family to oversee for their good and for his glory. This little family is meant to be a God-glorifying, disciple-making unit. As you repent throughout a lifetime, God's Word and God's Spirit will teach you how to better lead and love those in your household. And you will learn to lead with affection and authority. You will connect with your children, ensuring that you have their obedience and their hearts. In the process, you will become a man they both love and respect. Leading that little flock is glorious and self-sacrificial work.

At the same time, you are also developing the spiritual habits that Paul demonstrated in his fatherly care for his churches. Those were the same shepherding qualities he expected the leaders after him to exercise. This is the type of shepherd that is most effective in the church. They love others even as they understand that immaturity remains. They lead with patience, moving the sheep along to greener pasture. They are respected and loved. Godly shepherds have the heart of a child but a backbone of steel.

As you grow in relational wisdom, you will bless not only your household but God's household, the church. By his grace, you *can* lead both of your households well.

FOR REFLECTION AND APPLICATION

1. How does a well-led family glorify God?
2. Does your family have a posture of service toward the world and the church? Or have you and your wife fallen into a child-centered focus?
3. What do you think about the idea that God is preparing you to rule in eternity by training you to rule on earth? How does that encourage you and change how you look at your responsibilities?
4. How has God used this book in your life? What will be your biggest takeaways?
5. If you are a church leader, are you convinced that living the gospel at home is a fundamental aspect of godliness? What can you do to strengthen families in your church?

ACKNOWLEDGMENTS

Rejoice that your names are written in heaven. (Luke 10:20)

In many ways, the Bible is about names. From Moses desiring to know God's name to the angel revealing the name that is above every name, Scripture is deeply concerned with names. God chose to fill entire chapters of the Bible, such as 1 Chronicles 1 and Romans 16, with names. We don't know these people personally, but God does. And he takes time to acknowledge their contribution to redemptive history. Similarly, the following people may not be known to you, the reader, but they are vitally important to the work of this book. God will not forget their deeds (see Heb. 6:10). In this short section, I want to thank just a few people who have contributed to my life and this resource.

This book is from a pastor's heart, and it's primarily written for pastors. I so appreciate the faithful pastoring from Kevin McKay, Travis Rymer, and the other pastors and overseers of Grace Harbor Church who live out these principles. It has been a joy to work with you. Your willingness to let me teach the materials helped solidify some of these ideas. In addition, I am filled with hope and thankfulness as I survey a new generation of young pastors bringing the gospel to historic New England churches or new church plants.

A number of brothers and sisters have been tremendously supportive of the work of The Disciple-Making Parent ministry. It has been a joy to lock arms with you and minister out of the overflow of your friendship and prayers. Thank you to the Dalrymples, Mins, Hines, Bakers, Darlings, Bullocks, Distefanos, Hardings, Barlows, Hulberts, Ungerechts, Pearceys, Kings, Bonhams, Metaxatos, Priddles, Scotts, Pauls, and many, many more.

I am thankful for those who have evaluated some of the content of this book, including Travis Rymer, Dave Comeau, Dan Darling, Joel Sedam, and Daniel Howe.

Ed Stutz contributed in several unique ways to make this book possible.

Thank you also to Ruth Olsen and Melanie Makin for their many hours of editing and research.

Finally, to my family: A mere thank you is not sufficient for all that you have contributed to this. Kara, Chapman, Bekah, and Nate, you lived underneath my leadership with a joyful chaos. As adults, you dwell on the good and conveniently forget the mistakes. I look forward to watching you live out the gospel at home as you manage your own households to the glory of God. And to my wife and partner in ministry, Sharon, your patient endurance, belief in this calling, and constant love have made our journey a joy.

APPENDIX A

WHAT IS LEADERSHIP?

When the leaders lead in Israel, when the people volunteer, blessed be the Lord. (Judg. 5:2 CSB)

In the introduction, you met Jake, Ron, and Will as examples of poor leadership. But what specifically were they lacking? What exactly is leadership itself? We briefly discussed this topic in chapter 5. For something so important, many are unclear about it in their thinking. What is effective leadership? And more importantly, what is godly leadership? In this appendix, we will seek to understand the essence of godly and effective leadership.

DEFINING THE WIND

We all know poor leadership when we see it: lack of direction, lack of communication, lack of awareness, lack of wisdom, lack of passion, lack of decisiveness, lack of foresight, lack of confidence, and lack of connection with others. Poor leadership is easy to see.

But what makes for effective leadership? It is certainly not personality. Successful leaders look so different—tall, short, sports-lover, booklover, intellectual, emotional, hard-nosed, easygoing. There is no one leadership personality. Defining compelling leadership is a little like defining the wind. We know it when we see it, but trying to describe it is difficult.

Ultimately, effective leadership is influence. It is the ability to move others to do or be something different. That influence can be used for good or evil. A person can inspire others to great achievements for a glorious cause. Or that same influence can be used to harm others.

Having understood effective leadership, what is effective *godly* leadership?

THE GOOD SHEPHERD

In the Scriptures, the dominant metaphor for a leader is that of a shepherd.[1] A good shepherd embodies humility, care, tenderness, and courage. He feeds the sheep and defends them from their enemies. God described himself as Israel's shepherd, tenderly caring for his people. He promised one day to send a shepherd from the line of David. Of course, Jesus is this Great Shepherd. What a privilege to place ourselves under his watchful care!

The Great Shepherd also delegates some of his authority to undershepherds who are to lead and care for his flock in his name. Today, shepherding or pastoring has been equated with teaching, comforting, and counseling. But the word picture of shepherd also carries with it the concepts of initiating, deciding, and leading. The two, shepherd and leader, are combined. Thus, a shepherd is a leader.

GODLY LEADERSHIP

Having quickly surveyed the rich biblical imagery of a shepherd-leader, how do we actually carry out this kind of leadership? John Piper gives us a helpful definition of godly leadership, which I referenced

1. See, for example, Gen. 48:15; Pss. 23:1–4; 100:3; Isa. 40:11; Ezek. 34:23; John 10:11; and Heb. 13:20.

in chapter 5: "Spiritual leadership [is] knowing where God wants people to be and taking the initiative to use God's methods to get them there in reliance on God's power. The answer to where God wants people to be is in a spiritual condition and in a lifestyle that display his glory and honor his name."[2]

Let's look at that again slowly. Spiritual leadership is

- knowing where God wants people to be,
- taking the initiative to get them there,
- using God's methods,
- in reliance on God's power.

This is the essence of leading God's household and our family household.

It seems so simple . . . and yet it isn't. Describing a plane as having a body, two engines, two wings, and three wheels is very different from actually piloting an F-15 fighter jet. Mastering these different aspects of leadership is deeply complex work that takes a lifetime of growth. Simply put, leading well is easier said than done!

Whole books and courses teach the intricacies of leadership. I certainly don't expect that this one appendix will do more than scratch the surface. But with that in mind, I want to suggest several qualities of a maturing leader that we should keep in mind.

A MATURE LEADER KNOWS WHERE GOD WANTS HIS PEOPLE TO BE

Let's return to the first part of Piper's definition: "I define spiritual leadership as knowing where God wants people to be." To lead well, you need to be clear on where God wants his people to be. What sort of individual life and church life are we aiming for?

2. John Piper, "The Marks of a Spiritual Leader," Desiring God, January 1, 1995, www.desiringgod.org/articles/the-marks-of-a-spiritual-leader.

Paul had a similar understanding of leadership. He told the Philippian church that his continual presence was for their progress and joy in the faith (see Phil. 1:25). In other words, his goal was to move them where God wanted them to go. A quick study of the life of Paul reveals that he defined this progress as hearing and believing the gospel, gathering disciples together in churches, and growing in Christlikeness. He wanted to move them from immaturity to maturity.

Yet, like Paul, we are all merely Christ's undershepherds. Our time to help others grow is limited. Paul had been called to preach the message in regions beyond Philippi, and so he would leave that church before they had matured. Others like Apollos would follow behind and help these disciples take a few more steps toward maturity. Still different men, called to be elders, had a local ministry overseeing the new disciples with the same purpose—to mature God's people in the faith (see Acts 20).

All of these individuals saw where God's people were and where he wanted them to go. No matter what ministry role you have, a good leader is here for the progress and joy of the saints. He or she is taking the initiative to move God's people one step closer to where God wants them to be.

Convictions

Crucial to leading is not only knowing where God wants his people to be but being convinced that this is important. It's not enough to just have a belief; you must also hold motivating convictions. Dr. Albert Mohler writes, "Without convictions you might be able to manage, but you cannot really lead."[3]

Leaders can face two real dangers in this area. The first temptation is to have no real convictions about growth. These individuals are occupying an office but not moving people ahead. They are jellyfish floating with the tide.

3. Albert Mohler, *The Conviction to Lead: 25 Principles for Leadership That Matters* (Bethany House, 2012), 26.

The second temptation is to act on one's convictions unwisely. An immature leader takes godly principles and clumsily imposes them on others. He impatiently seeks to do too much too fast. He does not study the people God has given him to patiently bring them along. Convictions without wisdom result in a leader who is impulsive, argumentative, and bullheaded.

A mature leader, on the other hand, has core convictions derived from his study of the Word, the guidance of the Spirit, and the wisdom of mentors God has put in his life. His ministry principles are seasoned by spiritual and relational wisdom. Those beliefs continue to mature as he matures, reflects on what the Spirit is teaching him, and studies those underneath him. These convictions are the concrete foundations on which his ministry rests.

Leading *This* People in *This* Season

Convictions alone are not enough though. A godly leader must know where God wants *this people* to be. While some of what God wants for his people is timeless, other parts are not. A mature leader will realize that he has been given a particular group of people to watch over. He is not a generic pastor but an overseer of *these distinct* people. They will have unique strengths, weaknesses, personalities, hurts, and histories. Wise leaders, like wise husbands, dwell with their people in an understanding way (see 1 Peter 3:7). They are praying about how to apply God's principles to this people in this season. A wise leader studies the specific group the Lord has given to him.

A MATURE LEADER INITIATES USING GOD'S METHODS AND POWER

Let's return to the second part of Piper's definition: "I define spiritual leadership as . . . taking the initiative to use God's methods . . . in reliance on God's power."

A maturing leader takes the initiative. He is not reactive but proactive. God has charged him to care for his sheep and build the church.

He actively and prayerfully thinks about how to do that. Knowing where God wants individuals or groups is of no help if a leader will not step out in faith—that is, initiate.

But initiate what and how? Initiate using one of God's diverse methods in reliance on God's power. In many ways those God-ordained methods are the topics we covered in the second half of this book. When we think about the "how" of leading, we think about subjects like communication, goals, motivation, and management. This list does not even include other vital God-ordained means such as prayer.

However, two methods bear special mention in this appendix because they are so important, and they have not been emphasized in the book.

First and most profoundly, a Christian leader influences through the Word of God. Faith comes from hearing, and hearing through the Word of God (see Rom. 10:17). Leaders teach. If God calls us to lead in a pastoral or shepherding capacity, it will involve teaching the Word of God in some manner. That teaching may be in public, in a small group, or in counseling. It may be formal or informal. But we must never forget that the chief tool of the Spirit is the Word of God. All of us are commanded to "remember [our] leaders, who spoke the word of God to [us]" (Heb. 13:7 NIV). Leaders speak the Word of God. It is the primary means of changing God's people.

Second, God works through unique individuals. Yes, *you* are a way God works to change his people. God's Word tells us that pastors and teachers are gifts from Christ to his church (see Eph. 4:11–12). Just as each book of the Bible reflects the personality of the writer, so no two leaders oversee in the same way. God has put you in a specific time and place to influence people. You have unique gifts and talents as well as unique burdens and assignments from the Lord. You may be a five-talent leader or a two-talent leader. But God wants to work through you. Yes, *you*!

Becoming the leader he wants you to be means continually learning how God has designed you so that you are not neglecting your gift (see 1 Tim. 4:14). It also means learning how God has *not* designed you. You may be a visionary who cannot manage his way out of a cardboard box. Or you may be manager who, when given a task, faithfully brings it to completion. Or you may be some unique combination of both. Part of growing in effectiveness is gaining a deeper grasp of both your strengths and your limitations.

A MATURE LEADER KNOWS HE NEEDS MORE WISDOM

If I could add anything to Piper's definition, it would be the word *wisely*. Godly leadership is *wisely* knowing where God wants his people to be. It is *wisely* taking the initiative to move them there. Wisdom is the art of skillful living. It is weighing all the biblical information and knowing which principle to apply when, given the current situation. Leading well, whether in the church or the home, requires wisdom. And this is often what young shepherds lack. God wants to train you in leadership *wisdom*.

As Solomon began his reign, the Lord appeared to him in a dream and invited him to request anything. Solomon asked, "Give your servant therefore an understanding mind to govern your people, that I may discern between good and evil, for who is able to govern this your great people?" God was so pleased with his request that he declared Solomon would be the wisest person ever to live (1 Kings 3:9–10).

It was both Solomon's wise words *and* his wise leadership that spread his fame and brought God glory. After hearing the words of Solomon and seeing the accomplishments of his wise leadership, the queen of Sheba was left breathless, exclaiming what a blessing it was for her to hear his wisdom *and* for his men to live under his rule (1 Kings 10:1–10). Solomon's wise words and oversight glorified God and blessed his people.[4]

4. This theme of wise words and wise actions appears elsewhere in Scripture as well. For example, Luke emphasizes the mighty words and deeds of Jesus (see Acts 1:1) and Moses (see Acts 7:22).

If a leader's actions can bless people, his actions or inactions can also hurt them. Solomon prayed for wisdom so that he might administer justice. This implies that *a lack of wisdom in a leader results in feelings of injustice, and perhaps actual injustice, for those underneath him.* If you are wise in your priorities and in your methods, your leadership will bless others. When you lack wisdom, those underneath your care will feel it as injustice, *even if you have a good and sincere heart.*[5] For example, the church I pastored attempted to send out a number of individuals to plant another church. Some members made tremendous sacrifices. But because of a lack of wisdom in our leadership, this church plant did not flourish. Expectations were dashed, and trust was lost. While the leadership team had a pure motive, our lack of wisdom ended up hurting others. Good leadership has both integrity and skill. In this case, we lacked the skill. Realizing the power we have to both bless and injure should cause church leaders and household leaders to cry out for wisdom.

A MATURE LEADER IS AGGRESSIVELY TEACHABLE

Finally, a good spiritual leader is continually *growing* in that wisdom. One year, two US military officers and their families traveled quite a distance and joined our church. What struck me immediately was how teachable these two colonels were. They were enthusiastic servants and were always inviting feedback and asking questions. When I remarked to one about his attitude, he immediately responded, "In the military we call that being aggressively teachable. You will not go far in the US military as an officer unless you are aggressively teachable." If that is true of officers in the armed forces, how much more should it be true of officers in God's church!

5. See Chap Bettis, "Wisdom and Justice VS Lack of Wisdom and Injustice," The Disciple-Making Parent, accessed April 15, 2025, www.thedisciplemakingparent.com/wisdom-and-justice-lack-of-wisdom-and-injustice.

The higher we climb in leadership, the greater influence and visibility we will have. But with that greater influence comes a greater ability to hurt others through a lack of wisdom. In addition, we may find it easier to deflect criticism and critique. We may become thin-skinned and defensive. We may stop worrying about our blind spots. Jonathan Leeman has observed, "The more talented the man, the more humility he needs. The longer he serves, the more dangerous his pride can be."[6]

A stagnating leader, coasting on his accomplishments, becomes a target for sin and Satan. How do we avoid this trap? By being humble and taking responsibility to grow. Leadership entails a lifetime of lessons. A godly shepherd will seek to learn from each situation the Lord puts him in. It really is simple: If you aren't reflecting, you aren't growing. While he is confident in God's call on his life to lead the flock, a mature shepherd will also know that he has not arrived. He will remain aggressively teachable.

GROWING IN LEADERSHIP WISDOM

So far, we have seen that a godly leader needs to understand God's goals for his people, the methods he is to use, and the godly implementation of these methods. We might call this combination *leadership wisdom*. This wisdom involves the ability to size up a situation and know what is called for in the moment. It is knowing how to communicate and how not to communicate this direction. It is understanding a godly timetable given the resources God has given you. It is knowing when to speak and when to listen, what to say and not say. Leadership wisdom is a critical, though sometimes elusive, foundation for making good decisions by considering numerous factors.

6. Jonathan Leeman, *Authority: How Godly Rule Protects the Vulnerable, Strengthens Communities, and Promotes Human Flourishing* (Crossway, 2023), 119.

For example, I know of a young pastor who replaced the long-time founding pastor of a church. This new pastor came in with godly convictions concerning doctrine and church life. Unfortunately, he didn't take time to study what God had done in the church before. He attempted to make major changes quickly. His shepherding was clumsy. When approached by the other elders, he grew defensive. While he possessed knowledge, he did not have discernment. His doctrine and ecclesiology were pure, but he had a profound lack of leadership wisdom.

Some might call this sort of wisdom *emotional IQ*. It includes self-awareness, social awareness, and relational awareness. We might also call it situational awareness. The term *situational awareness* originated in the US Air Force in World War I. Pilots were taught to perceive, understand, and effectively respond to their situation. Pastors need this same aptitude. We need to recognize what God is doing in any given situation, understand its significance, and then decide how to act. A key indicator of whether any church leader will succeed in a ministry is how fast he can develop his situational awareness and applicable wisdom. Seminaries can train in *knowledge*, but imparting *wisdom* is a much harder task. Unfortunately, the leader described above did not realize his need to grow in this area. Both he and the congregation suffered.

How do we get the leadership wisdom we need? Some of it can be learned from asking older, wiser leaders or by reading. Much of it will come through real-life experiences and mistakes. But what if there were a smaller context than the church to learn about individuals and lead a group? What if God created a place for each of us to grow in communicating, motivating, teaching, discerning, encouraging, and correcting? What if God could put us in a smaller setting where there was more affection and forgiveness?

He did. It's called the family. That's why the subject of this book is so important. We lead well in the home so that we can grow in wisdom and lead well in the church.

CONCLUSION

Leadership means taking the initiative to move God's people where he wants them to be. Our Savior works through fallen sinners like you and me to shepherd his people. His perfect payment is sufficient for all our failures. But he also gives us the great privilege of shepherding others with increasing skill. This oversight is one way we express our love for him (see John 21:15–17). But in that great opportunity, we can bless the saints or hurt them. We need to aggressively grow in leadership wisdom so that we can be all that God intends us to be.

FOR REFLECTION AND APPLICATION

1. Have you ever tried to distill the essence of leadership before? How does Piper's definition help you in your own leadership?
2. Leaders are to help people move where God wants them to go. How knowledgeable are you about biblical patterns for sanctification or ecclesiology? How can you grow in these?
3. Analyze some good leaders you have served under. How have they lived out these principles of leadership?
4. Do you see why a lack of leadership wisdom can lead to feelings of injustice? How does that motivate you to grow in wisdom?
5. What do you think about the phrase "aggressively teachable"? Would you describe yourself this way? What could you change to be more aggressively teachable?

APPENDIX B

SELF-EVALUATION

The following survey will help you take the material in this book and apply it to yourself. However, conduct this self-evaluation in light of the gospel. No one is perfect. We all are growing in living out the gospel at home.

LOVING AND LEADING MY WIFE

I do not understand the biblical principles of marriage.	1	2	3	4	5	I am clear on the biblical principles of a marriage that honors the Lord.
I am passive. I neglect my marriage because of work or hobbies. Or I just coast along because my wife seems to do fine.	1	2	3	4	5	I actively take the initiative to build a marriage that honors the Lord.

I am insensitive to my wife and other women. I can be chauvinistic.	1	2	3	4	5	I am learning to value and understand my wife and other women more deeply.
I do not regularly talk with my wife. Or I get easily angered. I do not listen well to draw her out.	1	2	3	4	5	I am learning to skillfully communicate with my wife in a way in which she feels heard.
My wife and I do not talk about spiritual things or how she is doing spiritually.	1	2	3	4	5	I seek to encourage my wife spiritually.
I do not think of my wife as a teammate. I don't seek to develop her skills and gifts.	1	2	3	4	5	I seek to help my wife develop her skills and gifts.
I am not teachable. I am thin-skinned and defensive. I do not invite feedback.	1	2	3	4	5	I am able to receive critique from my wife and others.
We do not handle conflict in a healthy way. I seek to win, or I passively avoid conflict.	1	2	3	4	5	I lead us to talk through conflict in a healthy way.

I just give in so that my wife will be happy. I regularly respond to her initiative by saying, "Yes, dear."	1 2 3 4 5	I make hard decisions that are in everyone's best interest, even if they don't appreciate it at the time. I realize that I will give an account for what I agree to, and I am willing to be unpopular for a while.
My family is here to serve me. Or I substitute "helping out" for leading the family.	1 2 3 4 5	I seek to both die to myself as a servant and lead the family.

LOVING AND LEADING MY CHILDREN

I do not understand the biblical principles of parenting or my understanding is shallow. I just go with whatever my wife says.	1 2 3 4 5	I am clear on the biblical principles of parenting and know what God's Word says. I take the initiative to make sure my wife and I are on the same page.
I do not oppose disobedience. I do not have a real plan. I make excuses for my children. My wife takes care of the plan and the discipline.	1 2 3 4 5	I exercise my parental authority in a godly way. There are helpful consequences to correct behavior.

I am harsh or angry. I am emotionally disconnected.	1 2 3 4 5	I exercise my parental affection in a godly way. My children know that I love and care about them. There is joy in our house.
I push my children to present an image of good behavior. I do this because I want others to think well of me or think that we represent Christ well.	1 2 3 4 5	I know we are a family that needs the gospel. We can be real with each other, including being open about our failures. Honesty and authenticity are valued.
I am not tuned into how things are affecting my wife and children. My wife shoulders it all.	1 2 3 4 5	I am overseeing the whole household well. I am thinking about how we respond to outside challenges and commitments.
I do not communicate encouragement and vision to our whole family. I am silent or negative in this area.	1 2 3 4 5	I communicate well to our whole family, encouraging them and casting vision.
I am resigned to squabbles and fights.	1 2 3 4 5	I am teaching our children principles of unity and helping them to practice these principles.

I don't teach my children the gospel and the Bible. Or I teach in a boring manner. I am indifferent to their walk with the Lord.	1 2 3 4 5	I teach my children the gospel and the Bible. I am growing in my ability to explain it at their level. I am actively concerned that they give their lives to Jesus.
I have shallow interactions with my older children. I do not ask questions to understand their hearts.	1 2 3 4 5	I seek to speak more deeply to my older children, counseling them and defending them from threats. My counsel is increasingly gospel-rich.
My children are there to serve me.	1 2 3 4 5	I am learning to appropriately die to my own desires while leading.
I let social activities or school/sports activities crowd out our family's engagement with the church.	1 2 3 4 5	I guard our schedule so that our family can participate in corporate worship and build relationships with others in our church.

Our family is often late to the worship gathering, tired from staying up too late, or spiritually disinterested.	1 2 3 4 5	I help my family prepare for Sunday worship in practical ways.

LEADING THROUGH STORMS

I ignore trials that come upon our family. Or I am angry at my children for inconveniencing or embarrassing me.	1 2 3 4 5	I expect storms in this parenting journey. I lean into them with the proper balance of affection, authority, and authenticity.
I try to hide our problems and present our family as problem-free.	1 2 3 4 5	I invite others into our problems.

MINISTRY TO OTHERS

I am not committed to the local church. Our family comes first. I see the church as extraneous to my life and family.	1 2 3 4 5	I lead our family in commitment to the local church.
We do not serve others.	1 2 3 4 5	I lead our family to serve others.

My home is my castle. I rarely invite others in.	1 2 3 4 5	I lead our family to open our home in hospitality.

GENERAL ORDER

I am overspending. I don't know what our finances are. I am not giving.	1 2 3 4 5	I have made sure that our finances and spending are in order. I lead us to give.
I am not taking care of the possessions God has entrusted to me.	1 2 3 4 5	I am making sure that our car and our house are in good working order.
I regularly have to break my word, and I often don't keep my commitments.	1 2 3 4 5	I make sure to keep my verbal commitments. We are not overcommitted.
Our house is a constant mess.	1 2 3 4 5	Our house is generally in order.

APPENDIX C

A WIFE'S EVALUATION

This evaluation should be used carefully. No husband is perfect. We all need grace. Marriage is the union of two imperfect people, and a good marriage involves much forbearance and forgiveness. Nevertheless, your husband can benefit from your perspective. Your gracious but honest feedback concerning growth areas will be helpful.

LOVING AND LEADING YOU

My husband does not understand the biblical principles of marriage.	1	2	3	4	5	My husband is clear on the biblical principles of a marriage that honors the Lord.
My husband neglects our marriage because of work or hobbies. Or he just coasts along because I seem fine.	1	2	3	4	5	My husband actively takes the initiative to build a marriage that honors the Lord.

My husband is insensitive to me and other women. He can be chauvinistic.	1	2	3	4	5	My husband is learning to value and understand me and other women more deeply.
My husband doesn't regularly talk with me. Or he gets easily angered. He does not listen well to draw me out.	1	2	3	4	5	My husband is learning to skillfully communicate with me in a way in which I feel heard.
My husband does not talk to me about spiritual things or how I am doing spiritually.	1	2	3	4	5	My husband seeks to encourage me spiritually.
My husband does not think of me as a teammate. He doesn't seek to help me develop my skills and gifts.	1	2	3	4	5	My husband seeks to help me develop my skills and gifts.
My husband is not teachable. He is thin-skinned and defensive. He does not invite feedback.	1	2	3	4	5	My husband is able to receive critique from me and others.
We do not handle conflict in a healthy way. My husband seeks to win, or he passively avoids conflict.	1	2	3	4	5	My husband leads us to talk through conflict in a healthy way.

My husband gives in so that I will be happy. He regularly responds to my initiative by saying, "Yes, dear."	1 2 3 4 5	My husband makes hard decisions that are in everyone's best interest, even if I don't appreciate it at the time. He is willing to be unpopular for a while.
My husband thinks the family is here to serve him. Or he substitutes "helping out" with leading us.	1 2 3 4 5	My husband seeks to both die to himself as a servant and lead the family.

LOVING AND LEADING HIS CHILDREN

My husband does not understand the biblical principles of parenting, or his understanding is shallow. He just goes along with whatever I say.	1 2 3 4 5	My husband is clear on the biblical principles of parenting. He takes the initiative to make sure he and I are on the same page.
My husband does not oppose disobedience. We don't have a real plan. He makes excuses for the children. I take care of the plan and the discipline.	1 2 3 4 5	My husband exercises his parental authority in a godly way. There are helpful consequences to correct behavior.

My husband is harsh or angry. He is emotionally disconnected.	1	2	3	4	5	My husband exercises his parental affection in a godly way. Our children know that he loves and cares about them. There is joy in our house.
My husband pushes our children to present an image of good behavior.	1	2	3	4	5	My husband knows we are a family that needs the gospel. We can be real with each other, including being open about our failures. Honesty and authenticity are valued.
My husband is not tuned into how things are affecting me and the children. I shoulder it all.	1	2	3	4	5	My husband is overseeing the whole household well. He is thinking about how we respond to outside challenges and commitments.
My husband does not communicate encouragement and vision to our whole family. He is silent or negative in this area.	1	2	3	4	5	My husband communicates well to our whole family, encouraging us and casting vision.

My husband is resigned to squabbles and fights.	1	2	3	4	5	My husband is teaching our children principles of unity and helping them to practice these principles.
My husband doesn't teach our children the gospel and the Bible. Or he teaches in a boring manner. He is indifferent to their walk with the Lord.	1	2	3	4	5	My husband is teaching our children the gospel and the Bible. He is growing in his ability to explain it at their level. He is actively concerned that they give their lives to Jesus.
My husband has shallow interactions with my older children. He does not ask questions to understand their hearts.	1	2	3	4	5	My husband seeks to speak more deeply to our older children, counseling them and defending them from threats. His counsel is increasingly gospel-rich.
My husband thinks our children are there to serve him.	1	2	3	4	5	My husband is learning to appropriately die to his own desires while leading.

My husband lets social activities or school/sports activities crowd out our family's engagement with the church.	1 2 3 4 5	My husband guards our schedule so that our family can participate in corporate worship and build relationships with others in our church.
Our family is often late to the worship gathering, tired from staying up too late, or spiritually disinterested.	1 2 3 4 5	My husband helps our family prepare for Sunday worship in practical ways.

LEADING THROUGH STORMS

My husband ignores trials that come upon our family. Or he is angry at our children for inconveniencing or embarrassing him.	1 2 3 4 5	My husband leads through storms with the proper balance of affection, authority, and authenticity.
My husband tries to hide our problems and present our family as problem-free.	1 2 3 4 5	My husband invites others into our problems.

MINISTRY TO OTHERS

My husband is not committed to the local church. Our family comes first. He sees the church as extraneous to our family.	1	2	3	4	5	My husband leads our family in commitment to the local church.
We do not serve others.	1	2	3	4	5	My husband leads our family to serve others.
My husband's home is his castle. He rarely invites others in.	1	2	3	4	5	My husband leads our family to open our home in hospitality.

GENERAL ORDER

We are overspending. My husband doesn't know what our finances are. We are not giving.	1	2	3	4	5	My husband has made sure that our finances and spending are in order. He leads us to give.
We are not taking care of the possessions God has entrusted to us.	1	2	3	4	5	My husband is making sure that our car and our house are in good working order.

We regularly have to break our word, and we often don't keep our commitments.	1	2	3	4	5	My husband makes sure that we keep our verbal commitments. We are not overcommitted.
Our house is a constant mess.	1	2	3	4	5	Our house is generally in order.

RECOMMENDED RESOURCES

Bonus material is also available at www.thedisciplemakingparent.com/myhwbonuses. This includes a reproducible copy of the evaluations, suggested questions to ask a prospective pastor, and a short chapter for women.

See www.thedisciplemakingparent.com for more information about my books:

The Disciple-Making Parent: A Comprehensive Guidebook for Raising Your Children to Love and Follow Jesus Christ (Diamond Hill Publishing, 2016) equips you to evangelize and disciple your children.

Parenting with Patience: Overcoming Anger in the Home (Diamond Hill Publishing, 2019) teaches you how to grow in patience toward your spouse and children.

Parenting with Confidence: Biblical Truth in a Chaotic World (Diamond Hill Publishing, 2022) presents biblical teaching on foundational principles of parenting.

ALSO FROM P&R PUBLISHING

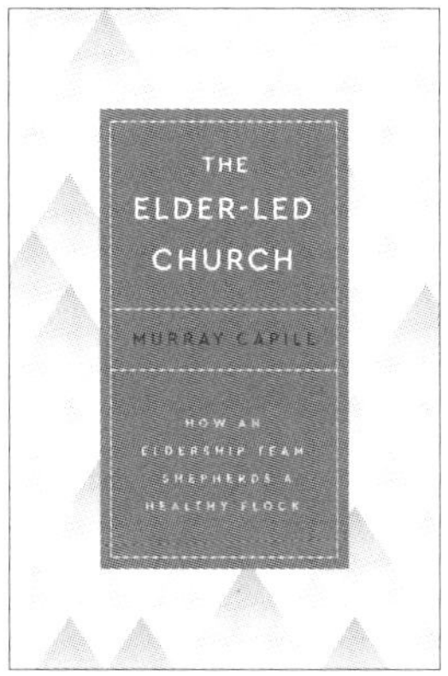

Church leadership is a shared responsibility, not a solo venture. This book equips pastors and elders to lead the church together as a team, focusing not so much on what they are to *be* but on what they as a body are to *do*. Written by a former pastor, now a seminary lecturer and longtime volunteer elder, this book is a groundbreaking resource for local churches of all shapes and sizes.

"An amazing achievement on eldership—a true gift to the church! This Christ-centered, gospel-focused, biblically grounded, theologically clear, exegetically thorough, well-researched, and immensely practical book should find its home in every church and seminary library and the hands of every man called to lead, oversee, shepherd, protect, and teach God's church."
—**Douglas Sean O'Donnell**, Senior VP of Bible Editorial, Crossway Books

ALSO FROM P&R PUBLISHING

Do you want to defend your faith but aren't sure where to begin? Mark Farnham's accessible guidebook simplifies apologetics and empowers Christians to effectively present the gospel in all its glory and rationality. This new edition includes practice case studies, chapter review questions, and a new chapter on engaging in gospel conversations over the long term.

"Marvelously clear, practical, and emboldening. Excellent guidance for anyone who seeks to be more faithful and effective in gospel advance."
—**Fred G. Zaspel**, Pastor, Reformed Baptist Church, Franconia, Pennsylvania

"One of the most down-to-earth, helpful books on apologetics that I have read."
—**Mark D. Allen**, Senior Fellow, Center for Apologetics and Cultural Engagement, Liberty University

Did you find this book helpful?
Consider writing a review online. We appreciate your feedback!

Or write to us at editorial@prpbooks.com.
We'd love to hear from you.